American Papers on Humanism and Religion

Alistair J. Sinclair Ph.D.

Published by
Almostic Publications
Glasgow

ISBN 978-0-9574044-0-3

Contents

Preface

This book comprises a miscellaneous collection of my papers and articles published or submitted for publication in American journals and magazines from 2009 to 2012. They are all on the subjects of humanism and religion. Some of them have been revised substantially from their original form. Their content follows on from arguments in my two published books: *What is Philosophy?* (Dunedin Academic Press, 2008), and *The Answers Lie Within Us*, (Ashgate Publishing, 1998). The following were originally published thus:

- "What to do About Religion: A Plan of Action." *Essays in the Philosophy of Humanism*, Vol. 17 (2), Fall-Winter 2009, pp. 35-42.

- "The Need to Complete the Secularization of Society." *Essays in the Philosophy of Humanism*, Vol. 18 (2), Fall-Winter 2010, pp. 25-35.

- "A Humanist's Faith: Towards a Humanist Alternative to Religion." This was first published as an online paper and is now much revised: Cf. http://www.essaysinhumanism.org/07sinclair.pdf

- "Dualism and Humanism." *Essays in the Philosophy of Humanism*, Vol. 19 (1), Spring-Summer 2011, pp. 41-56.

- "World One and the Loss of the Humanist Consensus." *Essays in the Philosophy of Humanism*, Vol. 19 (2), Fall-Winter 2011, pp. 43-60. This paper is also revised substantially.

- "Henry Ford: The Visionary Humanist." *Essays in the Philosophy of Humanism,* Vol. 20 (2), Fall -Winter, 2012), pp. 81-103. This paper has been re-edited and revised.

- "Posterity – An Eighteenth Century Answer to God and Religion." *The Humanist*, Vol. 71 (2), March/April 2011, pp. 39-40. Copious references have been to this article to render its content more scholarly.

The rest were submitted to American magazines at one time or another, but are otherwise unpublished in their present form. I thank the American Humanist Association for allowing me to reproduce the above EPH papers. I must also thank Marian Hillar, the founding editor of *Essays in the Philosophy of Humanism*, for his help and support in preparing and publishing the papers in EPH. I also want to thank Jennifer Bardi, editor of *The Humanist* for her encouragement and courtesy in publishing and dealing with the various articles I submitted to her.

Part One

Religion

I. What To Do About Religion
A Plan of Action

Abstract

In this paper, I argue that we can challenge religion in its own backyard by setting up community centres to wean local communities from their dependence on organized religions. This is a new departure not to be compared with most humanist societies which have a much narrower remit in promoting humanism itself. These centres may be based on humanist principles but no absolute conformity to these principles is required. Unlike religious organisations, there would be no need for orthodoxy or adherence to specific belief systems. Such centres are to be not purveyors of religion but explorers of the human condition in all its forms. They are to function as inclusive organisations rather than exclusive ones. All kinds of views and opinions would be considered and those that are disagreeable would not be excluded because they are unorthodox. By these means, we might at last inspire humanity to put religion behind it and move forward to pastures new.

Getting beyond religion

Humanists talk and write endlessly about religion but they don't do much about it. Though religion is shown with great clarity to be irrelevant in this day and age, not a lot happens as a result. It is supposed to be in decline but there is no sign of its imminent demise. If the hot air of constant debate could blast away religion, it would be long gone. Voltaire famously cried: *écrasez l'infâme!*[1] – 'crush the wretched thing!' or 'extinguish the abomination!'[2] But it hasn't gone away. In fact, by violently opposing people's religious beliefs we may strengthen them. We try to make people more rational who already believe themselves to be quite rational enough, thank you very much.

What therefore can we do about religion that does not make enemies of religious people? I think that we can to get beyond religion in a positive way that makes the humanist outlook attractive to the community without antagonising people unnecessarily. Getting beyond religion means making organized, hierarchical religion a thing of the past, not because it is forbidden but because people no longer need it. It entails replacing an authoritarian outlook, based on absolute belief, with a toleration of disbelief and of those with whom we disagree. It is not a matter of believing anything and everything. We want to create a climate of understanding in which belief is not accepted simply on authority and without question. Though there is a great deal in religion that is of immense value, the practice of religion is less acceptable. We may admire and wish to preserve the cultural contributions of religion such as the architecture, the music and much of the literature. But there is no longer any need in our society for practices that mesmerize people with   mindless rituals and repetitive mumbo-jumbo suggestive of obsessive compulsive disorder.

Let me clarify further what I mean by 'religion'. I take it to refer particularly to organized religion which imposes beliefs by authoritarian means, that is to say, by a hierarchical structure that wields authority by appealing to scripture, carrying out repetitive rituals and ceremonies, and manipulating people's emotions. A religion demands an absolute and unswerving faith, so that it involves belief more than understanding. It is dominated by an élite that imposes a fixed faith on their devoted adherents. As their jobs depend on their perpetuating the faith, they will defend it, by hook or by crook.

A religion usually has sacred scriptures that are inviolable to revision or alteration. In contrast, in so far as a humanist has any faith or belief, it is entirely his or her own and is constantly open to revision and upgrading in the light of new insights and understanding. Whereas religion consists in power over people, humanism is about power over ourselves. The former saves us the trouble of being ourselves whereas the latter shows us how to be ourselves. Religion belongs to our tribalistic past in which individuality was suppressed instead of nurtured.

Planning to take over

We surely need a plan of action if we are ever to get beyond religion. I suggest that we steal its thunder and render it socially and culturally unnecessary in a concrete and practical way. But how do we do this? Humanists already perform ceremonies for marriages and deaths. Community centres could be set up countrywide to rival what churches of one sort or other already do. They would systematically fulfil all the social and community functions currently undertaken by religious centres. Their activities would attract no more than the competitive rivalry that exists between neighbouring supermarkets, restaurants and the like.

Churches, chapels, synagogues and the rest are all exclusive centres to which you must belong in a formal sense. Non-believers are either excluded from their proceedings or can make no contribution to their activities. In contrast, humanist centres can be inclusive ones which include potentially the whole community without exception. They would be capable of doing more for the community than churches because they are interested in the community as a whole. They have no prior perspective or hidden agenda that motivates their activities.

Such centres might perform ceremonies of birth, marriage and death, and organize conventions, fairs and pageants commemorating the history, people and traditions of the community. These practices would help to establish the identity and unity of the community. They could organize regular meetings to explore and discuss religious matters without being associated with any particular religion. These meetings would facilitate the formation of informed beliefs and opinions through teaching rather than preaching. Facilitators would initiate and encourage debate and discussion without telling anyone what to think. Basic qualifications for such facilitators could include a degree in philosophy.

The ultimate aim would be to make it unnecessary for people to attend the traditional churches since community centres would do all that they require without demanding adherence to any particular religion. Given time, churches and other religious centres might be taken over without having to destroy or replace anything in religion that is of universal value and interest. The culture of religion in the form of its literature, music, and architecture would be preserved but not its authoritarian, ritualistic or hierarchical aspects.

Humanist principles but not humanist ideology

Community centres may be organized according to humanist principles but not humanist ideology. These principles would include the pursuit of open-minded inquiry, toleration of differing opinions, and eschewing of prejudicial or dogmatic thinking. Above all, such centres would avoid the imposition of an orthodoxy of beliefs to which everyone is supposed to conform. The only admissible orthodoxy lies not in anyone's beliefs but in the humanist principles which themselves cannot be pursued dogmatically without self-contradiction. Constant criticism and examination of any beliefs would ensure that none of them could become 'orthodox' or enforced in preference to all other beliefs.

Sadly, humanism itself is prone to ideological extremes, as it can be the source of orthodox beliefs which are as unsubstantiated as any religious beliefs. For example, the equality between human beings might be enforced dogmatically as opposed to a celebration of their differences. The relativism of beliefs may also be pursued dogmatically making it impossible to take any beliefs seriously or acknowledge that some beliefs are truer than others. The truth of beliefs is obviously a very important source of perpetual discussion and inquiry. Complete scepticism of all beliefs would make superfluous all such discussion and inquiry. Thus, the ideal of generally accepted scientific truth would be paramount as far as any truth seeking is concerned.

Most humanist organisations are more concerned with preserving orthodox humanism rather than with replacing religion in people's hearts and minds. They rightly fear that the humanist heritage might be lost. Their attitude is one of a retrenchment since they cannot match the aggressive proselytising of religion. Such defensiveness means that humanism is becoming a rearguard activity which is slowly retreating before the forces of superstition and fundamentalism.

Thus, Robert D. Finch argues that the humanist legacy is not only under attack from religious fundamentalism but is also at the mercy of "our own dysfunctional organisations."[3] But his solution is to provide more of the same in developing and propagating humanist ideology, and in imposing humanist orthodoxy. "Thus, Humanists need to spend time in celebration, extolling the virtues of Humanism. We should feel happily convinced that Humanism provides the best way to live."[4] In arguing that all humanist organisations should have the same beliefs and aims, Finch could lapse into the frame of mind that the Emperor Theodosius adopted in imposing Christianity by military force throughout the Roman Empire in 380 CE.[5] We need to avoid the aggressive imposition of orthodoxy, if we are to get beyond religion altogether.

In his book, *Living Without Religion*, Paul Kurtz seems also to offer a humanist orthodoxy in place of religion. He advocates a form of humanist philosophy which he calls 'eupraxsophy'. Though this singularly unattractive name is unlikely to appeal to the public, Kurtz nevertheless suggests that 'eupraxsophy centers' are needed, in spite of secular objections such as the following:

> A strong atheist would deny any need for a center. He is so opposed to the baneful effects of dogmatic religion that he does not wish to create analogous institutions. He sees no point to prayer or ritual. There is no need for clergy. Why perpetuate the superstitions of the past? Why build secular humanist centers or edifices? [6]

In reply, Kurtz thinks that "There is a need for an institution in society that will provide some wisdom in life."[7] However, he advocates what seems to be an educational centre rather than a centre dedicated to serving its local community as religious centres do. If we are get beyond religion, we need community centres which will do everything that the churches do plus the educational aspect that Kurtz proposes.

Winning hearts and minds

If these new centres are to win the hearts and minds of their respective communities, they must offer more than secularism pure and simple. Neither a relativistic toleration of all beliefs nor an advocacy of no belief whatsoever is enough. There has to be something more than drab, materialistic atheism with which to regale the community. We will only get beyond religion by going along with it to some extent. We must enthuse people about something out of the ordinary otherwise we will have nothing to say that interests people. Unless we capture their imagination and arouse their deepest feelings about the important things in life, we will surely fail.

Elsewhere in this book I argue that a humanist can have a faith at least as strong as any religious faith. (See section three below on "A Humanist's Faith: Towards a Humanist Alternative to Religion") If humanism is to replace religion in people's affections, it must be broadminded enough to embrace our ideal aspirations and not oppose or ignore them altogether. In my view, we require a broad view of humanism that includes the possibility of a humanist faith. We are not thereby making an ideology or religion of humanism. A humanist faith is our own and is not imposed on us in an authoritarian manner. This use of the word 'faith', when applied to humanists, is indistinguishable from belief. Indeed, in languages such as German and Greek, one word (*Glaube* and *pistis*, respectively) is used to refer to both faith and belief. The distinction arose from the use of the Latin *fides* originally meaning 'trust' or 'confidence' to refer to those who put absolute trust in Christ and hence the Christian church in its many forms. There is no room for such absolutism in the humanist outlook. Our beliefs depend on evidence and on constant criticism of them.

What to do in practice

We need to wean people away from religion by strengthening those aspects of humanism that are not wholly incompatible with the religious outlook. We can, for example, focus on the ethos of the community and of humanity as being humanist ideals that bring us together in a non-mystical and non-supernatural way. Such en ethos is what we all have in common when we all come together to get things done and to celebrate the achievements and aspirations of our communities, organizations and ultimately humanity as a whole.

Community centres can therefore embody the ethos of the community in a practical and non-mystical way. They might use local traditions such as the celebrated Groundhog Day in Punxsutawney, Pennsylvania[8] to help us to unite the present with the past without commitment to religious doctrines of any kind. An even more outstanding example of a community unified by a local tradition is the annual Up-Helly-Aa fire festival in Lerwick in the Shetland Isles.[9] This tradition is largely a late 19th century invention based loosely on the Norse traditions of the islands. Significantly, it has become an isolated tradition rather than a revival of pagan Norse religion. It has proved to be hugely popular and an excellent tourist attraction.

Such traditions give unity and identity of purpose to the whole community in the way that religious centres have often aspired to do but by using inhuman ideals and unattainable divine aspirations. This unity is required nowadays because religion is divisive and true believers may take up arms in the name of their respective beliefs. Strong believers are prone to give meaning to their empty lives by fighting those with equally strong but incompatible beliefs. If humanists do not assert themselves by supplying a coherent alternative to religion, such sectarian conflict seems inevitable in the long run.

These community centres ought to be self-financing charities within their respective communities. They should be free to organize themselves to serve their communities appropriately. Each centre can find its own way to represent what is best and worthwhile in the ethos of its community. No two centres would be the same in the lectures, courses, discussions, ceremonies, recreations or whatever activities that they consider appropriate, rewarding and uplifting to offer their respective communities.

Perhaps there would also be an opportunity for wealthy individuals who are prepared to support such centres. They might be encouraged to do so by having centres named after them. This could be their bid for immortality and it would also encourage them to get involved with their respective communities, just as soccer club owners engage with their clubs. This is not an unusual proposal as all kinds of charitable organisations adopt the names of individuals: schools, hospitals and universities and their buildings are often named after wealthy benefactors. However, there is no need for these centres to be named after people already well known to the public. Richard Dawkins, for example, is presumably famous enough not to need anything named after him!

The ethos of the community

Local humanist organisations tend not to think in community terms. They are social clubs concerned mainly with discussing humanist theory and subjects of humanistic interest. We need to make a fresh start with humanist centres based on community needs. They should be unifying organisations. To that effect, they need to take account of the ethos of the community in which they are based.

It is arguable that a community in the form of a neighbourhood, village or district has an ethos distinct to itself when its inhabitants identify strongly with it. They have interests and activities in common which bring them together and make the community more meaningful to them than it is otherwise. The ethos is manifested when they come together physically in meetings and when they recognize what they have in common as a community. Their inner will as individuals are both raised and augmented as a result. They find more reasons within themselves to get together with others to do worthwhile things. This aspect of the ethos is important because our constant involvement in a community of our fellow human beings provides external limitations to the ethos. Contributing to the community disciplines our inner development and ensures that it grows and develops meaningfully and purposefully. In partaking of the ethos of the community we find a sense of belonging that is essential to our well-being and personal development.

These centres can rally the community by appealing to tradition and history rather than religion and authority. Religion is admissible only in so far as it forms part of that tradition and provides valuable insight into the human condition. It is no longer admissible as a body of ultimate or absolute truth commanding obedience and submission.

The ethos of humanity

We participate in the ethos of humanity whenever we empathize with our fellow human beings when they are afflicted by famines, earthquakes, tsunamis, terrorist attacks and so on. It is an additional dimension of ourselves and an expression of our human feelings. It is not the same as the idea of humanity which has been misused by utopian ideologists to justify killing and torturing their fellow human beings. In that case, the idea has become more important than people and is treated in an absolutist way. In contrast, the ethos of humanity is not above and beyond us but an intimate part of what we are as individuals. It is more concerned with our sympathetic feelings about other people than with what we think of them.

The ethos of humanity is particularly important in uniting us as a species against the racial, national, religious, sectarian or economic divisions that forever threaten to turn us against each other in self-destructive war and conflict. The slogan, *Amate l'Umanità!*, (love humanity!) was used by the great Italian patriot, Giuseppe Mazzini (1805-1872), in his campaign to unify the disparate nations and city states of Italy.[10] He considered the interests of humanity to be more important than those of family and country. The creation of a united Italy was more vital to humanity than loyalty to smaller units which were perpetually in conflict with each other. Another example is the 18th century Scottish Enlightenment. Its whole ethos consisted in a regard for humanity which arose when the identity of the Scottish nation was subsumed into that of Great Britain with the union of parliaments in 1707. That regard for humanity made sense of the loss of Scottish identity. The Scots saw that their greater duty lay in serving humanity with their literary, scientific, architectural and other efforts, and that this was worth sacrificing national identity.

The future of humanism

Being a humanist should be no different from being a human being. Indeed, humanism in the form of human rights has become the prime civilizing influence throughout the world. But the sad fact is that humanism is often criticized nowadays as if it were an ideology rather than a loose body of opinions about the human condition. Perhaps the future of humanism lies in focusing on the more general topic of the human ethos in the form of the inner being that we develop within ourselves.[11] This is a subject for debate and argument rather than belief. Those who reject the topic out of hand cannot avoid thinking about the problems and puzzles which it raises concerning the human condition.

In developing the human ethos within ourselves we identify more completely with all humanity and with life forms in general. We empathize with the plight of our fellow human beings and indeed our fellow living beings throughout the world. Developing that inner ethos requires self-discipline and self-knowledge. It is not a soft option. The human ethos has infinite possibilities ahead of it as long as we all learn sufficient self-control to keep it on the straight and narrow. We don't require religion to discipline us since we can reach within ourselves to find the inner strength needed to do whatever is required to ensure our future. Dwelling on that ethos does not make us self-centred and selfish as long as we are using the notion to broaden our thinking and to think about others at least as much as we think of ourselves. Only by developing our thinking in this way can we understand better our place in the universe so that we achieve modesty and magnanimity as a result.

The thankless task of convincing recalcitrant individuals that they can save themselves has always been the burden of humanists everywhere. To that end, humanism is an open-ended viewpoint as long it involves constantly exploring the human ethos, the ethos of the community and the ethos of humanity. Its ultimate aim must be to finally convert the world from religion and bring humanity into a new state of enlightenment.

Notes and References

1. Voltaire's Letter to Jean le Rond d'Alembert, 28th November 1762 ': "Quoi que vous fassiez, écrasez l'infâme, et aimez qui vous aime." Whatever you do, crush the infamous thing, and love those who love you. This was written in reference to crushing superstition, and the words "écrasez l'infâme" ("Crush the Infamy") became a motto strongly identified with Voltaire.

2. Thomas Carlyle's translation of Voltaire's saying as in *The French Revolution*, Vol. I, Book 2, Ch. VIII. Cf. this Classic Reader site: http://www.classicreader.com/book/106/12/ *Accessed 2012-09-01*

3. Robert D. Finch, 'The Humanist Legacy: Preservation, Improvement and Promotion,' *Essays in the Philosophy of Humanism*, Vol. 14, 2006, p. 29

4. *Ibid.* p. 30.

5. Cf. Marian Hillar's quotations from the Codex Theodosius in 'Servetus and the Switch to the Humanistic Social Paradigm,' *Essays in the Philosophy of Humanism*, Vol. 15, 2007, pp. 94-95.

6. Paul Kurtz, *Living Without Religion: Eupraxsophy*, New York: Prometheus Books, 1994, V, p. 149.

7. *Ibid.* p. 150.

8. Cf. this 'Groundhog Day' site: http://www.groundhog.org/groundhog-day/ *Accessed 2012-09-01*

9. Cf. this Shetland tourist site: http://visit.shetland.org/ under 'Up-helly-aa'. *Accessed 2012-09-01*

10. Giuseppe Mazzini, *The Duties of Man*, London: J.M. Dent & Co. pp. 49-50.

11. This was the subject of my first book, *The Answers Lie Within Us*, (Ashgate Publishing, 1998), though this was very much a preliminary and tentative study which is now the subject of a completely different book which outlines our duality mentality.

II. The Need to Complete the Secularization of Society

Abstract

It is argued here that our future depends on our completing the secularization of society. This means addressing the problem of authoritarian religions that suppress freedom of belief and opinion. We must promote a post-religious humanism to deal with this problem. This is no more than reviving the humanist consensus which all the major religions acknowledged at least till the 1970s. Until then a comparative religion movement sought to construct a world religion but its endeavours have come to nothing. Secularization means that religious sentiments belong to individuals who work them out for themselves. These sentiments are no longer the prerogative of organisations that impose them on individuals. It is for everyone to develop their own creed on humanist principles. This humanist message contributes to a world monoculture which is now being established everywhere and on which the world's future peace and security depends.

What the secularization of society involves

The secularization of society will only be completed when post-religious humanism consigns authoritarian religion to the history books. Extreme secularization advocates getting rid of religion altogether but this has been tried in communist countries and has proved to be impractical. Moderate secularization consists only in reforming religious organizations so that they embrace post-religious humanism. What is required of them is that they no longer proselytize their respective religions as if there were no alternatives to them or no truths other than those preached in their religion. Religious organisations are anti-humanist in restricting people's freedom of thought and opinion by doing their thinking for them and by requiring adherence to forms of clothing and behaviour that may be offensive to the rest of society.

A free society is one in which no one is compelled to identify him or herself so completely with any group or organisation that they lose their identity and self-respect in the process. In so far as a religious sect or organisation is authoritarian and anti-humanist, it demands absolute and unqualified obedience from its members. It deprives them of their freedom to think for themselves. There is therefore no room for such organizations in a free society.

Secularization means bringing religious organizations into the community so that they are they no longer at odds with other organizations but contribute equally to the community as a whole. It means that they adopt humanist values more wholeheartedly than previously. The community centres, which I advocate in the last section above on 'What to do About Religion', are models that show how post-religious humanism can function in the community without any authoritarian or proselytising intent. As a result, there would no longer be particular religions but only religious views and sentiments which are held by individuals for themselves alone. Religion is not abolished but humanized.

Thus, post-religious humanism goes beyond religion by humanizing people's religious views and sentiments which are the prerogative of individuals and not of organizations enforcing them. There is no longer any need for an organization to preach doctrines to be believed absolutely and without qualification. This stipulation is an inevitable and necessary development as we cannot move forward as a species while we are divided against each other by absolute and irreconcilable religions that scorn the contributions of other religions. We need to eliminate extremist thinking which causes harmful conflict and violence by introducing unnecessary hatred and enmity. We have to make it clear that this way of thinking is unacceptable and that each individual must recognize these propensities within themselves and deal with them accordingly. This paper examines how western society has progressed in this secularization process and why it is necessary to pursue to its ultimate conclusion.

Reviving the humanist consensus

What is proposed here is not radical or revolutionary. It only means reviving the humanist consensus which prevailed in western society until the 1970s. The fundamentalist view of religion was discredited until then and the major religions were in a process of secularizing themselves. The humanist consensus made such secularizing reforms inevitable. Thus, for example, Roman Catholic Church's reforms in the Second Vatican Council (1962-1965) led to priests and nuns being able to wear secular clothing and to services being held in the vernacular language instead of Latin. The Catholic Church was in the process of emerging from its medievalism and entering the modern world. Unfortunately, there has been an obvious backsliding from this advance.

Until the 1970s, western culture prevailed generally even in Islamic countries: archive films of the streets of major cities such as Cairo show that everyone was wearing fashionable western clothing. Head covering was nowhere to be seen. From then on, the humanist consensus was gradually lost. Conflicts in places like Northern Ireland and the Middle East were fuelled by religious bigotry which steadily grew and culminated in the events such as 9/11. The 1979 Iranian revolution brought a reaction against the humanist consensus which was attributed to western influence instead of being regarded as an enlightened advance in our view of the human condition. There can be no end to this desecularizing descent into barbarism unless humanism reasserts itself and continues the secularisation of society.

The historical vulnerability of humanism

Historically, humanism has been a frail and transient thing that lasts only for brief periods. It is a delicate plant that requires constant nurturing and fighting for to maintain its hold. It is vulnerable when its message is diluted and it becomes identified with scepticism and relativism. People can put up with uncertainties only for a short period before their yearning for certainties brings authority and tyranny flooding back. The humanist message needs to be constantly reinforced and restated to show that it has a sure and certain view of our future. We must reiterate the reliability and inevitability of this message and make it as much a part of society as, for instance, human rights has become. Humanists must therefore get their act together and show the world that it can well do without religion in the traditional sense of the word.

History shows that when religious people hold their beliefs lightly and non-dogmatically then they can appreciate the value of science and philosophy, and even contribute to their development. This has happened during periods of intellectual ferment, such as in Islamic Spain between the tenth and eleventh centuries, and in Christian Europe during the twelfth century, the Renaissance and the Enlightenment periods, when science and philosophy were actively promoted by clerics and the religious authorities. At other times, such as during the Dark Ages and the Counter-Reformation, extreme views concerning the primacy of religion led to the discouragement and suppression of philosophy and scientific research by religious authorities.

For example, Copernicus was a Catholic priest who was encouraged by his ecclesiastical superiors in his astronomical researches which showed that the Earth goes round the Sun. However, the next generation of clerics retreated into a defensive and dogmatic fundamentalism in the wake of the Reformation and its challenge to Rome's supreme authority. They were fearful of the consequences to their religious doctrines of innovative scientific thinking. As a result, Galileo's support for the Copernican view was suppressed by the Catholic authorities, and thereafter scientific thinking was discouraged in Catholic countries.

Another example is Thomas Reid (1710-1796) who was an ordained Minister of the Church of Scotland before he lectured in philosophy and Newtonian science at Aberdeen University. He rose to the challenge of David Hume's sceptical views and founded Scottish common sense movement in philosophy. He also laid the foundations for the science of psychology in his book, *An Inquiry into the Human Mind* (1764), which also anticipates non-Euclidean geometry.[1]

These examples show that religion is not inherently incompatible with science and philosophy. It only becomes so when its doctrines are taken to extremes and enforced rigidly and dogmatically. Indeed, both science and philosophy can also be taken to dogmatic extremes in the form of scientism and the various ideologies such as communism.

Most forms of religious extremism arise when the irrational, emotional side of religion is over-emphasized. The irrationalities of religion are often cited as an attraction rather than deterrence. When something makes no sense and is 'irrational', this is far from being a commendation. It should spur us to find out why it makes no sense rather than give up thinking about it altogether. Senseless beliefs can poison the mind and encourage the uncritical reception of lies and deception, as for instance in some politicians' bigoted belief in the existence of WMD in Iraq against all the evidence. When we stop inquiring into things and criticizing them, our knowledge and understanding of things stagnates. Post-religious humanism therefore aims to keep inquiry open on all matters relating to religion.

Post-religious humanism rationalizes religious-mindedness by showing how it contributes as much to our knowledge and understanding as do science and philosophy. Whatever succeeds religion should make more sense than existing religions in the same way that Christianity was more rational than the Olympian religions which it superseded in the Roman Empire from the late 4th century CE onwards.

For example, the letters of St. Paul are arguably more rational and philosophical than the mythologies of the Olympian religions. He sets out the doctrines of Christianity very clearly and cogently in these letters. Indeed, St. Augustine concluded that Christianity made more sense to him than its Manichean rival because he could defend its doctrines against the objections of Manicheans. In book five of his *Confessions*, St. Augustine rejects Manichean doctrines about the stars because they were incompatible with the scientific facts established by the expert astronomers of his day.[2] He found in Christianity what he considered to be the most rational religion available in his day. Thus, the rationality of Christianity was more important in establishing its dominance than any intuitive revelations, mystical or other irrational elements. Indeed, the early Church succeeded in suppressing the mystical elements represented by Gnosticism. This alone contributed to its rationality. However, that was 1700 years ago and scientific advances now put the rationality of Christianity and other religions into question. Surely, we now deserve something better than a reversion to such archaic attempts to give meaning to our lives.

Why post-religious humanism is necessary today

Post-religious humanism is necessary to ensure the future progress of humanity. We now live in a global monoculture in which the key divisions are those of the individual person and humanity as a whole. All the ephemeral divisions of race, religion and nationality are becoming outdated as increasing globalization moves us beyond them. The races are being increasingly mixed up and difficult to discern. Religions can no longer claim a monopoly of truth without conflicting in a hostile way with other religions and with society as a whole. Nations are becoming increasingly integrated through trade and commerce, political and economic alliances, communications, transportation, and the ubiquity of the internet.

In today's 'global village'[3] absolute differences between us can no longer be tolerated if recurring war, violence and unnecessary conflict are to be avoided. If we are to have any kind of future, then what unites us as human beings must take precedence over what divides and sets us against each other unnecessarily. We live in a world where absolute exclusivity is inadmissible. We are all at one in solving the serious problems that the world as a whole faces at this time.

Thus, the answer to the world's problems is not **multi**culturalism but **mono**culturalism. In today's increasingly integrated world culture, there is room for only one culture and that is the culture of the whole human race. Only one culture is now being established throughout the world as it gradually absorbs all cultural differences into itself. This is exemplified by the European Union which is currently absorbing nations with diverse cultures and languages. The fact that nations are still queuing up to join the EU in spite of the current economic difficulties is proof of its success and the necessity of its achievements. It is now virtually inconceivable that EU nations declare war on each other as in the 20th century and before. This cannot be said of other nations which are currently arming themselves and sizing each other up in a manner alarmingly similar to European nations pre-World War One. The promotion of this monoculture in place of all other divisions is therefore necessary to ensure our future security and the peace of the world.

Post-religious humanism contributes to the virtually unstoppable development of a global monoculture by integrating all religious views and inspirited sentiments. It entails the complete secularization of society which, as argued above, means religious views and sentiments contribute to society as a whole. They are no longer treated as 'otherworldly' or separate from everything else in society. As a result, everyone will acknowledge the absurdity of adhering to one religion as if it had all the answers and had a monopoly on truth.

Post-religious humanism is not itself a religion since it has moved beyond religion by absorbing its lessons, knowledge and wisdom. It recognizes the need to develop our inner being so that we are more in tune with humanity and the universe. This view transcends religion by making us more rational and commonsensical than is possible in the context of any religious organization, sect or cult. The lessons of all religions and philosophies are absorbed in this development of inner being. This humanist view applies to individuals and to all humanity, and is not held exclusively. It cannot be used to pit people against each other as religion often is.

What is here called 'inner being' includes those subjective feelings that are often interpreted as being religious but they are not exclusive to any particular religion. All beliefs are entertained without focusing on any particular one. It therefore goes beyond all the traditional religions in repudiating their authoritarian imposition of beliefs. It tells no one what they must believe or even that they must believe in anything at all.

There are at least three ways of dealing with any particular religion. (1) We can have a personal, scholarly or participatory interest in it. (2) We may be interested in it only at the personal level as we might be interested in any other human activity. (3) We may take a scholarly interest in which we study it in some depth without actually becoming an adherent. But a participatory interest means become an adherent and accepting all the doctrines, rituals and other requirement that makes one into a Christian, Jew, Scientologist or whatever. Such an interest may also include the personal and scholarly interests but it goes beyond these by enslaving the individual to the religion. Only the other two ways of dealing with religion are humanistically admissible. The personal and scholarly interests put religion at arm's length instead of enslaving us to it. Post-religious humanism encourages these interests and discourages the participatory interest where it involves an authoritarian hold over the individual. However, it is clear that the comparative religion movement of the 20th century embodied the view of post-religious humanism in discouraging the latter in favour of the ideal of a world religion, as is now discussed.

The failure of the comparative religion movement

The possibility of post-religious humanism began with the comparative religion movement which attempted unsuccessfully to lay the foundations for a unified world religion. Until the 1970s, this unifying aim of comparative religion was generally believed to be the obvious way forward for all the world religions. The following quotations taken from books on Islam and Hinduism show that this belief was widely accepted during the 20th century: The first is taken from a book by W. M. Watt called *Islamic Philosophy and Theology* and published in 1962:

> Each of the great religious communities is in closer contact with the other great religions than has ever been the case before. Members of the great religions are being forced, as never before, to learn how to live alongside adherents of other faiths. Consequently there are strong pressures

urging men towards a unified world religion. Ideally all that is of value in the several religions should be taken up into this one religion; but it is possible that to begin with humanity may fall far short of this ideal, and in this way much of value may be lost. The new problem for Islamic theologians, as for those of all the religions (including Christianity) is to present what they see of value in their religion in such a form that it is capable of being assimilated by others. The present survey has been written from the standpoint that there is much of value in Islam; and it would be thus a loss for the whole world if what is valuable is not transmuted and sublimated, and so made suitable for inclusion in the unified religion for the whole world.[4]

A remarkably similar view was expressed by Radhakrishnan in his book, *The Hindu View of Life*, first published in 1927:

The different religions are slowly learning to hold out hands of friendship to each other in every part of the world. The parliaments of religions and conferences and congresses of liberal thinkers of all creeds promote mutual understanding and harmony. The study of comparative religion is developing a fairer attitude to other religions. It is impressing on us the fundamental unity of all religions by pointing out that the genius of the people, the spirit of the age and the need of the hour determine the emphasis in each religion. We are learning to think clearly about the interrelations of religions. We tend to look upon different religions not as incompatibles but as complementaries, and so indispensable to each other for the realisation of the common end. Closer contact with other religions has dispelled the belief that only this or that religion has produced men of courage and patience, self-denying love and creative energy. Every great religion has cured its followers of the swell of passion, the thrust of desire and the blindness of temper. The crudest religion seems to have its place in the cosmic scheme, for gorgeous flowers justify the muddy roots from which they spring.[5]

The above passages express the ideal of the comparative religion movement, namely, that an examination of all the religions leads quite naturally to a unified world religion. They show that this movement was not just confined to Christianity and that it was widespread at least until the 1960s. The comparative religion movement began in the 1870s with the attempts of scholars such as Max Müller[6] and C.P. Tiele[7] to establish a 'science of religion'. It was not strictly a response to Darwin's *Origin of Species*, published in 1859; it was more a response to the increasing knowledge of and interest in religions throughout the world. The movement continued to gather pace during the 20th century, and perhaps its most popular exposition was in A.C. Bouquet's book, *Comparative Religion*, published in 1941.[8] Although Bouquet was a prominent Anglican clergyman and academic, his book contains a remarkably dispassionate account of all the religions including Christianity. His avowed aim was to pinpoint the common features of all the various religions as a prelude to unifying religion in general. This is an eclectic view which gathers together all the religions without supplying a conceptual system to which they can all be referred.

The movement was ultimately unsuccessful because its aims were too diffuse and it lacked a unified system of thought. Due to this lack of intellectual rigour, the comparative religion movement petered out during the 1960s, and the traditional religions gradually rediscovered themselves as Wittgensteinian 'forms of life'. They now see themselves as being independent and self-subsistent contributions to human culture. Instead of unifying themselves in the common interest of humanity, they are now engaged in a post-modern dialogue of mutual incomprehension. While religious leaders indulge in a high-minded deference to each other's beliefs, serious-minded fundamentalists of all faiths find more direct means of enforcing their beliefs on others. This can only lead to a tribalization of human belief systems in place of the unifying ideals of the comparative religion movement. Such divisiveness seems to go against the current trend by which we are overcoming our racial and national divisions to emphasize what we have in common rather than what divides us. The potential for conflict and war between competing religious blocs will remain while fundamentalists continue to preach the absolute truth of their respective religions compared with other religions whose adherents are equally convinced of the absolute truth of theirs.

How post-religious humanism goes beyond eclecticism and syncretism

The comparative religion movement failed because it led to a cataloguing and classifying of religions rather than the formation of something new which goes beyond all religions. It was an **eclectic** enterprize which studied all religions without discriminating between them. Such eclecticism provides no conceptual system by which the various religions can be compared and contrasted. In the end, it merely shows (1) how distinctive each religion is and (2) how difficult it is to reconcile them all into one unified religion. They simply continue on their individual paths without hope or desire for convergence or reconciliation between them.

At the other extreme, the **syncretist** approach combines one or more religions in an attempt to incorporate them. In effect a new religion results, as in the case of Sikhism which combines elements of Islam and Hinduism. Sikhism was not successful in replacing its constituent religions, any more than Islam has successfully replaced Judaism or Christianity. Perhaps the most striking example of all is the religion of Baha'i which set out as a syncretic religion including all other religions, as this *Encyclopaedia Britannica* article shows:

> Baha`i faith, religion founded in Iran in the mid-19th century by Mirza Hoseyn 'Ali Nuri, who is known as Baha` Ullah (Arabic: "Glory of God"). The cornerstone of Baha`i belief is the conviction that Baha` Ullah and his forerunner, who was known as the Bab, were manifestations of God, who in his essence is unknowable. The principal Baha`i tenets are the essential unity of all religions and the unity of humanity. Baha`is believe that all the founders of the world's great religions have been manifestations of God and agents of a progressive divine plan for the education of the human race. Despite their apparent differences, the world's great religions, according to the Baha`is, teach an identical truth. Baha` Ullah's peculiar function was to overcome the disunity of religions and establish a universal faith. Baha`is believe in the oneness of humanity and devote themselves to the abolition of racial, class, and religious prejudices. The great bulk of Baha`i teachings is concerned with social ethics; the faith has no priesthood and does not observe ritual forms in its worship.

As most people today have never heard of the Baha'i faith, we can confidently say that it has failed thus far in its mission of unifying all religions. Indeed, the more a religion strives to unify all religions in a systematic way, the more it is certain to fail because it becomes just another religion self-confidently proselytising itself as a religion. It merely adds to the sum-total of religious faiths. This includes Richard Dawkins' ill-advized attempt to replace religion with a biological view of things in *The God Delusion*.

Neither eclecticism nor syncretism can solve the problem of getting beyond all religions whatsoever to provide something recognisably better. It is here suggested that a system of thought is required which is broad enough to encompass all religious beliefs without being a religion. Post-religious humanism provides a philosophical standpoint within which all religious beliefs may be understood in their own rights. Religious extremism cannot occur when people learn to hold their beliefs at arm's length instead of regarding them as the absolute, unanswerable truth. However, a basic humanist's creed may be required to show that faith is not the prerogative of religion alone, as is now suggested.

The Need for a Creed

Our future both as individuals and as a species depends on our believing in ourselves but only in a qualified and self-critical way, in other words, in a self-reflective way. We must constantly examine and re-examine our self-belief so that we can move forward and fulfill our goals and purposes in life. To that end, we can devise a stable creed based on that self-belief. Without such a creed, we have no standpoint from which to evaluate our actions, aims and purposes.

Thus, many of us seem to need a basic creed to live by; a creed that is practical, sensible and down-to-earth and that gives us confidence in what we are as mere human beings and in what we can do collectively as a species. It should help us to do things rather than just accept things as they are. We need to think positively about ourselves and our prospects so that we can move on and embrace the future with confidence rather than dwelling on past failings and disappointments.

The need for a basic and fundamental creed may be fulfilled if it is universal enough to have characteristics such as the following:

- It can be embraced by all believers without necessarily threatening particular beliefs.
- It must go beyond all previous religious creeds while being practical, sensible and down-to-earth.
- It should give us confidence in what we are as mere human beings and in what we can do collectively as a species. We need to think positively about ourselves and our prospects so that we can move on and embrace the future with confidence rather than dwelling on past failings and disappointments.
- It should therefore help us to do things rather than just accept things as they are. In that respect it will differ from religious creeds which typically promote passivity and obedience.

The suggested Humanist's Creed below is an example of one humanist's creed. It is up to each individual to devise their own. This particular one does not expect any more from anyone than what we normally do in making something of our lives. It involves having faith in ourselves, in humanity and in power of human reason. But this faith needs constant reinforcement by our understanding and criticizing what it means and how valid and applicable it is in our daily lives. In that respect, it has a practical and educational role to play rather than a sacred or ritualistic role. For the humanist would rather teach than preach, and not tell people **what** to think but **how** to think. None of the beliefs in this Creed are the whole truth of the matter, but they can help each of us to strive towards the truth in our own way. They are not themselves the way but they illuminate our way.

A Humanist's Creed may help us in our daily lives to have confidence in our place in the world, in the power of reason, in the value of our fellow human beings, and in value of life in all its varieties. In contrast, a religious belief, such as a belief in the resurrection of Jesus Christ, or in the power of prayer, may lack practical application in daily life. Such beliefs are a distraction and do not help us to get things done. Moreover, such a creed is the minimal belief system that can apply to us no matter what other beliefs, religious or non-religious that we may espouse over and above these beliefs. Thus, one particular humanist's faith is summed up as follows:

A Humanist's Creed

The Strength of Knowledge

My faith is mightier than any religion because it is open-ended and founded on ever-increasing knowledge and understanding of what I am, what other people mean to me, and what life and the universe mean to me. The more I understand these things, the more interest I have in them and the more value and significance I can bestow on them.

The Power of Critical Reasoning

I have faith in the power of critical reasoning to reach truth, foster goodness, and promote justice, and I will conduct a personal quest for all these and will settle for nothing less. I will constantly strive to understand life's mysteries, as far as humanly possible, and will not be content with myths, absurdities, or similar fruitless or baseless deviations from truth. I will seek the good within me and within others and will fight for justice and sweet reason for as long as I have the strength and will to do so.

The Capabilities of Humanity

I have faith in the capabilities of humanity, notwithstanding its obvious fallibilities. My belief in its future is not unqualified, as it depends on humanity doing enough to ensure that future. If no one believes in its future then it has no future. I have faith that humanity is capable of saving itself and the planet if it makes sufficient effort to do so.

The Resilience of the Human Spirit

I have faith in the resilience and persistence of the human spirit which has already accomplished so much against all the odds. I believe that the spirit within us will prosper for as long as we nurture it and make the most of its potential for good and well-being.

The Uniqueness of Each Individual

I have faith in the potential of every human being to enrich the world with the uniqueness and originality of their contributions to it. I wish to see that uniqueness blossom forth in the right social conditions and thereby justify the existence of humanity both to itself, life and the universe at large.

The Possibilities of Life

I have faith in the possibilities of life which are limited only by the paucity of human imagination. I believe that life on Earth has secure foundations while the human race believes in itself and its mission to further life and limit damage to the planet. This requires each of us to make the most of our lives within the limits of our unique potential. In so doing, we serve the purposes of life as much as we are the custodians of it.

Notes and References

1. Cf. Thomas Reid, *An Inquiry into the Human Mind on the Principles of Common Sense*, in *The Works of Thomas Reid*, ed. Sir W. Hamilton, 8th Edition, Edinburgh: James Thin, 1895, Ch. VI, Sect. IX, pp. 147b-152a.

2. Cf. St. Augustine, *Confessions*, trans. R.S. Pine-Coffin, London: Penguin Books, 1968, Book V, Section 7, p. 98.

3. "With instant electric technology, the globe itself can never again be more than a village." Marshall McLuhan, *Understanding Media*, 1964, London: Sphere Books, 1968, Part II, ch. 32, p. 366. He first used the term 'global village' in *The Gutenberg Galaxy: The Making of Typographic* Man, Toronto: University of Toronto Press, 1962, p. 31.

4. W. M. Watt, *Islamic Philosophy and Theology*, Edinburgh University Press, 1962, p. 178.

5. Radhakrishnan, *The Hindu View of Life*, 1927 - London: Unwin Books, 1960, p. 43.

6. Cf. Friedrich Max Müller (1823-1900), *Lectures on the Origin and Growth of Religion as Illustrated by the Religions of India (1878)*

7. Cf. Cornelis Petrus Tiele (1830-1902), *Outlines of the History of Religion: to the Spread of the Universal Religions,* (1877), trans. J. E. Carpenter

8. A.C. Bouquet, *Comparative Religion*, London: Penguin Books, 1941.

III. A Humanist's Faith:
Towards a Humanist Alternative to Religion

*Man is that noble endogenous plant which grows, like the palm,
from within without.*

R. W. Emerson[1]

Introductory Remarks

It is not necessary to be religious in order to have a faith. I argue here that a faith based on humanism is stronger than any religious faith as it is self critical and based on not only reason but also on reality, evidence, scientific knowledge and plain good sense. Most religious faiths are mysterious and unfathomable because they hark back to a prescientific era of ignorance and superstition. But humanism offers a rational faith wholly compatible with the scientific advances in our outlook. So far from believing in anything or nothing, the humanist believes strictly in what appeals to his critical judgment and in what is really the case. In so far as the religious person believes in senseless, groundless things, there is no limit to what he may or may not believe.

A religion demands absolute and unswerving faith, whereas a humanist's faith is entirely his or her own. A religion requires a hierarchical structure with an élite that imposes a fixed faith on their devoted adherents. It usually has sacred scriptures that are inviolable to revision or alteration. In contrast, a humanist's faith is constantly open to revision and upgrading in the light of new insights and understanding.
Whereas religion consists in power over people, humanism is about power over oneself. The former saves people the trouble of being themselves whereas the latter shows them how to be themselves. Religion belongs to our tribalistic past in which individuality was suppressed instead of nurtured. It relies more on incontrovertible taboos than on self-referential morality and individual responsibility.

Therefore, humanism does not enforce particular beliefs and humanists are obliged to work out for themselves what they believe in or don't believe in. Their faith is such that they need no exclusive hierarchy or holy scripture telling them what to think. What follows exemplifies the faith of many humanists. It does not necessarily apply to all humanists, though hopefully it will aid them in strengthening their own particular faiths, if they have any. Not having any faith whatsoever is also compatible with being a secular humanist.

The word 'faith' when applied to humanists is indistinguishable from belief. Indeed, in languages such as German and Greek, one word (*Glaube* and *pistis*, respectively) is used to refer to both faith and belief. The distinction arose from the use of the Latin *fidēs*, originally meaning 'trust' or 'confidence', to refer to those who put absolute trust in Christ and hence in the Christian church in its many forms. The word *fidēs* became 'faith' in English and it was no longer enough merely to believe in Christianity; it was necessary also to have an absolute and unqualified faith in it – preferably a mindless faith. (A cowed congregation made the job of clergy so much easier!) There is no room for such absolutism in the humanist outlook.

Religious faiths appeal to the heart whereas humanism seems only to appeal to the head. But humanists only appear cold-hearted and dispassionate because they believe that the head must rule the heart. Reason also involves passion, and the more convinced that we are of the reasonableness of our beliefs the more passionate we are about them. Hence the fanaticism of true believers. The humanist is also passionate about his beliefs but he believes in keeping them within the bounds of good sense. He keeps them at arm's length to remain objective about them. His passions are muted because he leaves his beliefs open to further consideration. The mindset of a humanist is to expect and accept limitations to all his beliefs. Also, he does not approve of the authoritarian dictation of beliefs by any person or organization as he insists on thinking things through for himself.[2]

Humanism is sometimes blamed for the excesses of 20th century atheistic regimes. But it is a mistake to equate humanism with atheism. Not all humanists are atheists. There may be Christian, Jewish and Moslem humanists who hold their beliefs with humanistic understanding rather than religious rigour. Not all atheists are humanists. Hitler and Stalin were certainly not humanists. Marx ceased to be a humanist when he wrote the Communist Manifesto which advocated a dictatorship of the proletariat with its abolition of property and other inhuman acts that were recently put into practice by Pol Pot and his infamous regime in Cambodia. Such ideologies become religious faiths dominated by god-like personalities, and there is nothing humanistic about them. Since humanism is incompatible with tyranny, oppression, violence, and arbitrary acts of war, it offers a truly humane faith.

Firstly, a humanist's faith may be firmly grounded on reasonable beliefs concerning the reality of life, nature, and the universe. Secondly, it may depend on reasoned self-belief and belief in other people and society in general. Thirdly, his faith is strong and resilient because it is critically self-referential, especially compared with the uncritical faith of the typical religious believer. Fourthly, his belief in humanity can be based on rational and critical grounds rather than dogmatic and absolutist grounds. Thus, the strength of the humanist's belief comes from within. It results from philosophical and mental development rather than unquestioned conformity to a faith in which one happens to be born. This essay summarizes my own views, though I may have unconsciously imbibed many of them from sources now forgotten.

1. Belief in Life, Nature and the Universe

Caring About Life

Humanists have been unjustly criticized for their arrogance and speciesism. They are alleged to put human concerns above those of animals and living creatures in general. In fact, a concern for non-human species is an inextricable part of being a humanist. The humanist cares for all forms of life because he values life in all its variety. It is anathema to him to think that other life forms exist only to be exploited by human beings. Firstly, in being a self-reflective person, he cannot live with himself knowing that he has been callous and unjust towards his fellow living beings. Secondly, he believes in keeping his interests and concerns in perspective so that he does not make too much of our human interests relative to those of other life forms and *vice versa*. Both these aspects of the humanist view are discussed further in the relevant sections below.

Furthermore, as human beings we belong to the animal kingdom and have an abiding interest in it, as is evidenced by the sciences of zoology, botany, and biology. This scientific knowledge makes us care about non-human species and feel responsible for them. Our lives would be all the duller and more boring without such diversions. Thus, the humanist's belief in humanity involves taking account of the interests of other living species. It is in our interests to preserve the diversity of species on this planet and to propagate life throughout the universe. Fulfilling this role gives meaning and purpose to our activities and for that reason it is an inextricable part of the humanist outlook. The problem lies in keeping all these interests and concerns in perspective, as is discussed below in section four of this paper.

At one extreme we are nothing but animals and at the other extreme anything but animals. We either debase ourselves or over-exult ourselves in relation to other animals. Nihilists, cynics and sceptics typically take the former view and reduce us to the lowest common denominator. Religious minded people take the latter view and elevate us to scions of divinity. This view makes too much of the good and evil in us and renders us either angels or demons, with no grey areas between. In the humanist's view, we are much more than mere animals, not because we have divine attributes but because we have duties, obligations and responsibilities to ourselves, to other animals and to life in general. We are special animals because we are custodians of this planet whether we like it or not. We are also special in being able to make sense of life and the universe as a whole, however inadequately we are doing so at this time. As mentioned below, we also differ from animals in being able to celebrate our differences, even though we are also prone to suppress them through fear and lack of understanding of them.

The Reality of Life and Nature

The humanist believes in the reality of life and living. The fact that we live at all, suggests that life is not for nothing. What we make of it is everything. When we fail to make anything of life, it amounts to nothing. The humanist may reasonably say to himself: "I really live therefore I cannot escape the need to do something with my life if I am not to live in vain." He is responsible for his own life and he is beholden to no one and nothing for what he decides to do with it. Thus, his faith in himself and his future depends on his own efforts to justify his own existence and make something worthwhile of his life. In short, he believes that we are here to make the most of our lives, each of us in our own ways. We know this because there is nothing else for us to do with our lives.

William James said: "Believe that life **is** worth living, and your belief will help create the fact".[3] But this is not enough as the humanist requires reasons for his beliefs. He finds these reasons, for instance, in valuing life and its possibilities, and in caring about people and the problems facing humanity. Our own lives, the lives of other people, and the lives of living beings in general are valuable in themselves, because of the many reasons we have for believing them to be valuable. These reasons include the fact that we exist at all, and the fact that we can do something with our lives that interests us and makes us feel that we have not lived in vain. Our belief in the value of life also gives direction to the overall affairs of humanity. The preservation and furtherance of life on this planet and elsewhere is obviously an important role for humanity to play.

Nature both nurtures us and challenges us. It nurtures us with its bountiful supplies that enable us to adapt to the most unlikely conditions. It challenges us by its indifference to our existence on this planet, by its wasteful destruction of life through death and random catastrophes, and by its squandering of energy through entropy. The humanist does not believe in worshipping nature but in learning to live with it and adapt to it. He believes in the reality of nurturing nature of which we are an inextricable part. This belief is reasonable because we need to live in harmony with nature to ensure our survival as a species. In communing with nature we become at one with it. We are as much nature's product as sticks and stones and grass and grouse. We have a right to be here not merely because we **are** here, but also because we are produced by the same natural processes as everything else on the planet. But we differ from other living beings in that we only fit into the scheme of things by making a big effort to fit in. The humanist has faith in our ability to take our rightful place in nature, provided we work hard enough to ensure that we do. While it is natural for us to believe in ourselves, it is equally natural for us to give up and self-destruct. The choice is ours alone.

With our knowledge and technology, we now have the ability to nurture nature and take care of life on this planet. But we need wisdom and judgment to exercize our nurturing powers for the best possible purposes. The humanist believes that we can acquire sufficient wisdom and judgment as long as we learn to behave ourselves responsibly and thoughtfully. A thoroughly humanistic education system can accomplish this by aiming to help everyone to take the broadest possible view of everything in place of the narrow parochialism of religion and ideology. Such narrow-mindedness all too often puts us out of touch with nature because it makes us destructive of ourselves and our fellow creatures by setting us against each other.

The Creativity of the Universe
The universe composes all the matter and energy that has organized itself into the natural entities and processes surrounding us. The humanist believes not only in the reality of the universe but also in its creative power. He appreciates its potential to create ever more organized and purposeful life forms by its physical processes. Our scientific knowledge of the universe's capabilities gives us the power and responsibility to facilitate its potential for generating and sustaining life. Believing in the universe also means believing in the need to propagate life throughout the universe. We can also consolidate our place in the universe by interacting with it and by our relentless and endless quest to know and understand it.

The humanist believes that though the universe has no meaning or purpose, it does not exist for nothing. In so far as it exists for anything, it exists to be something. That something can be used by us to justify the fact of its existence. As a mere composite of matter and energy, the universe amounts to nothing and serves no purpose in itself. However, its creative and organizational processes make something out of matter and energy that is more than nothing. Its capacity for self-organization redeems it and makes it something. Its creativity in producing complex, living beings ensures that they have the power within them to justify the universe's existence by what they do with their lives. They are something rather than nothing in existing meaningfully and in finding meaning and acting purposefully in the universe itself. Only living beings are capable of justifying its existence by their meaningful and purposeful activities. We and other living beings add to the rationale of the universe by furthering our reasonable goals such as propagating life. As far as we know with any certainty, nothing else exists that can make sense of the universe and therefore justify its existence. Thus, in justifying our existence we *ipso facto* justify the universe's existence. In a purposeless universe, our purpose in life is to bring meaning into the universe which otherwise lacks meaning. This opportunity makes us a very important and indispensable species. Without us there is nothing else in the universe (as far as we know) capable of appreciating its majesty and its mystery.

Life and Death

The humanist's faith is based on the joy of our living at all. Life is a fabulous gift we have received from no one and from nowhere against all the odds. The creative processes of the universe produced us indifferently without mind or purpose and by pure chance. As Dawkins puts it: "It is overwhelmingly probable that you are dead."[4] Having won the celestial lottery by living even for a limited period of time, it is surely greedy and arrogant to desire the prolongation of that life for an eternity.

Yet death is not necessarily the end of everything for the humanist. He can believe in the reality of eternity into which everything is ultimately subsumed. The material universe subsists within time but outside time there is an everlastingness to everything that has happened within time. The conservation of energy suggests that nothing is lost forever in the universe, even though the mechanisms by which everything is preserved forever are not entirely known to us at this time. All that we can see at the moment is the entropic run-down of the material universe. There is evidently much more to be discovered and understood about what is happening in the universe. Meanwhile, we can believe that while we live, the events of our lives are embedded timelessly into the fabric of the universe never to be erased by any future physical events.

The fact that we are physically destroyed by death does not mean that the lives we have lived in time are at all destructible from an eternal point of view. Thus, as physical beings, we come from nothing and revert to nothing when we die, but our intervening lives are forever. They are our gratuitous gifts to eternity in return for the gratuitous gift of life. All this is mystical enough for the humanist without contravening common sense or current scientific understanding of the matter. He does not need to resort to supernatural or far-fetched explanations to explain such matters within the bounds of current knowledge. Anything more is best left to the fertile imaginations of science fiction writers.

2. Belief in Self, Other People and Society

The humanist is acutely aware of being nothing more than a fallible human being. He typically tries to make no more of himself than is supported by the reality of his talents and abilities. A realistic belief in himself requires him to balance his pride and humility. If he is too full of himself or thinks too little of himself, he won't deserve to make his mark on the world. It is as self-destructive to lack faith in ourselves as it is to have too much. Having a balanced view of ourselves means believing in what we can do with our lives, actually or potentially. Belief in our own potentialities presupposes knowledge of what we are and what we can or cannot do with ourselves. The humanist believes that realistic self-belief is reinforced by education, self-improvement, and self-direction. His self-belief is also curbed by his self-knowledge which helps to make him a principled and self-reliant person. He knows the very worst that he can think of doing but he doesn't do it on a point of principle and not because he feels coerced to do so.

The humanist lives with himself all the more easily because he appreciates other people's points of view whether he agrees with them or not. He is not constantly at loggerheads with them just because he doesn't agree with them. On the contrary, disagreements contribute to his self-knowledge and to his interest in other people as individuals. He needs such differences to make anything worthwhile of himself. Such relationships contribute to his self-preservation and self-expression. He cares about each individual because they are valuable and unique in themselves, regardless of how different they are from him. He believes in reasoning with people and disapproves of using fear and emotion to intimidate them into believing things.

Thus, the reality of other people and our relationships with them is confirmed by the value and love we bestow on them. They reciprocate with the value and love they confer on us in return. In having faith in other people we care for them and go beyond our selfish interests. We derive such moral standards as trust, sincerity, understanding, and sympathy from that faith. We cannot reasonably expect any higher moral standards from other people than we expect from ourselves. Therefore, we learn to be as trustworthy, sincere and sympathetic towards others as we expect them to be towards us.

The humanist also believes that our society has a future provided that we do enough to ensure its future. That future depends on its flexibility and openness to further change and development. The humanist wishes to maintain the openness of society by constant appreciation of opposing points of view, in other words, by means of critical self-reference.

3. Belief in Critical Self-Reference

Humanists seemingly tolerate every kind of behaviour because it is 'human' and 'anything goes'. But this superficial view overlooks the highly moral standpoint also implicit in humanism. In having faith in the potential of human beings, the humanist must put stringent demands on himself and on others to justify such a faith. He disciplines himself and expects others to behave in a disciplined manner because without self-discipline and self-restraint we cannot realize our human potential.

Unlike many religious people, the humanist relies heavily on critical self-reference to monitor his behaviour and that of others. This kind of self-reference is not the same as selfishness or self-centredness. It consists in self-knowledge of our strengths and weaknesses. We endeavour to understand other people on their terms as well as our own. We put ourselves in other's shoes, empathize with other life-forms, and broaden our outlook generally. With critical self-reference, we can look into ourselves and examine ourselves critically and dispassionately. We acknowledge our defects and shortcomings by embracing other perspectives and contexts and making them a part of ourselves. We move beyond our immediate selfish needs to take a full account of other's needs. We become bigger people in the process.

Critical self-reference makes us responsible for ourselves and requires us to think for ourselves. We learn to behave ourselves because we want to and not because external authority requires our absolute submission without further thought on the matter. This is a self-regulating morality instead of one imposed on us by external authorities who think they know what's good for us.

Our faith in ourselves is only justified when we are continually practising critical self-reference to improve ourselves and to avoid doing harm to others. Thus, self-reference aids self-knowledge and increases our awareness of what we are and what we can do. We strengthen ourselves within while becoming more acutely aware of how weak and vulnerable we are in the face of external events. This inner strengthening can be inculcated through the education system. It involves teaching rather than preaching. Humanistic education introduces us to the intellectual tools that we need to make the best of ourselves in society. Criminally or pathologically minded people who spurn such tools arguably suffer from a form of social sickness which is potentially curable by means of personal education sufficiently tuned to their needs and to deal with their pathological deficiencies.[5] A prison system based on retribution and rehabilitation is liable to be insufficiently organized to perform such an educational service. The humanist way is surely to punish the person rather than the crime, thus addressing the true source of the crime. (See my e-book on that subject entitled *Punish the Person, Not the Crime.*)

A humanist's faith is stronger and more reliable than any religious faith because it is based on open-minded rather than dogmatic principles. It relies not on absolute belief but on knowledge and understanding, and on the critical reasoning that self-reference requires. There is no room for dogmatic principles since all humanist principles are subject to constant review and criticism by means of self-reference. Where there can be no certainty, suspension of belief is preferable to belief for its own sake.

Unless our beliefs are tinged with scepticism, we may not adapt fast enough in response to new facts and new ways of thinking concerning our plight on this planet. Such open-mindedness made scientific advances possible in the first place, and religious injunctions that command absolute belief are incompatible with it. For example, if we believe absolutely that God will protect us no matter what we do then this belief will prevent us from being realistic about our place in the universe. Such a belief is not only incompatible with the scientific view of the universe but also prevents us from doing what needs to be done to prolong life on this planet.

The strength of this humanist faith depends on our doing things to justify our own faith to ourselves rather than simply believing things because others say so. In other words, we don't need to appeal to other people or to self-styled authorities to reinforce our faith. We must reach within ourselves to justify having faith. In so doing, we appreciate the value of humanity, duly qualified by an understanding of self, other people, and our place in the universe generally.

4. Belief in Humanity and its Future

The Growing Unity of Humanity

The humanist believes in humanity in a realistic way that does not involve putting it on a pedestal or worshipping it. The fact that he worries about its future does not mean that he makes too much of it. He cares about humanity because he belongs to it whether he likes it or not. This sense of belonging makes him interested in everything that is going on. And the more interest he finds in human affairs, the greater his sense of belonging. He is interested in the differences between people because these make us human as distinct from animals that are significantly less differentiated in form and behaviour. Our differences are important because they contribute to the dynamism of humanism. Our future depends on all kinds of people making their futures in their own way.

The humanist also believes that we are all the same in being different from each other. These are not just any differences, but only those that make sense to us and others. We are always answerable to others for our differences from them. But what we have in common as human beings is more important than that which divides us. We need each other not only for love or friendship but also because we are interested in each other's differences. We fall out with each other most when we try to make everyone the same as ourselves. This particularly happens when we fall into an authoritarian frame of mind in which we demand total agreement and submission from other people. The humanist believes in a 'live and let live' policy that allows others to get on with their lives even though their way of life is personally objectionable to him. It takes 'all sorts to make a world' but we also need to make a world in which all sorts can thrive.

The humanist therefore believes that our future depends on our pulling together to make a better future for the whole human race. The 'global village' of intercommunication and economic dependence unites us as never before. We must put behind us the absolute and outmoded differences between people based on race, culture, religion, politics, and nationality that divide us tribally instead of individually. These are largely historical fabrications that we won't really need in the fullness of time.[6] Even racial distinctions are on their way to extinction; a few generations of global intermixture will make racial boundaries impossible to discern. National divisions are being rendered obsolete by the European Union which unifies nations without threatening their sovereignty or cultural peculiarities.

The alternative is to descend into the internecine, self-destructive quarrels amongst ourselves to which we are all too easily prone when we try to eradicate our differences instead of celebrating them. If we are to avoid the wars, enmities and tribal divisions of the past, we must not forget our allegiance to the human race as a whole. If we care nothing about the human race as a whole, we don't deserve to have a future. Also, the impossibility of reconciling our individual strivings with those of humanity as a whole, makes for the unstable dynamism of humanity. We can at least be united in our diverse struggles for self-expression. Each individual has become virtually a species unto themselves instead of an undifferentiated unit of the human race. Such differentiation is driven by increasing cultural diversity and not by genetic variation. There is after all less genetic variation among human beings anywhere in the world than there is within a troop of chimpanzees.[7]

The humanist believes that our unified future depends on our allegiance to humanity overriding tribal allegiances based on authoritarian compliance. These allegiances erode our individuality by overemphasising our sameness, whereas open-ended organizations use our individual differences to further their social aims such as providing goods and services, or teaching facts and skills. Such organizations serve humanity by taking their rational place in the social order. By doing so, they help to bind us all together in a mutually beneficial social and economic nexus. Adam Smith's 'invisible hand' involves not narrow self-interest but enlightened, contextualized self-interest. It means being sympathetic to people rather than using powerful and emotional influences to intimidate people. Unless our organizations are sympathetic towards us and actively nurture our talents and abilities, they will simply stunt our growth as useful persons.

This process of unifying us and our organizations in relation to the needs and aspirations of humanity goes beyond multicultural plurality of the sort that tolerates cultures absolutely distinct from each other and from humanity as a whole. It means transcending all the superficial and ephemeral divisions of the past, to produce a world view which is common to all humanity and which respects the differences between individuals. There is simply no place for outdated cultures that hold people back and prevent them from joining the global culture as a whole.

Thus, humanity does have a future in so far as we individually and collectively recognize the importance of our unity and diversity as a species and make the most of that unity and diversity to ensure our future. We will have no future if we do nothing when we can at least strive for this unity and diversity. Our future is always in our own hands because we have the foresight and insight required to do something about it, however inadequate that may or may not be in practice. The external threats to the future of humanity, such as the occurrence of comets, pandemics, earthquakes, global warming or ice ages, will certainly overwhelm us if we are not unified enough in our resolve to overcome whatever misfortunes befall us.

Keeping Humanity in Perspective

The humanist does not believe in overvaluing or worshipping humanity. He believes in keeping it firmly in perspective and not making too much of it. His concern for the human race as a whole is important to him but it is only one perspective among many. His unending daily challenge is to reconcile all his concerns and worries, both personal and impersonal, as they only make sense within their respective contexts.

We keep our notion of humanity in perspective by not treating it so abstractly that it is above criticism. In other words, we treat it sceptically as a self-referential notion that refers back to us as fallible human beings. Whatever we do in the name of humanity is not always the right thing to do and we must be vigilant and exercise judgment in its application. Our belief in humanity is just as prone to inhuman extremes as, for instance, a belief in God. Those who believe fervently in humanity may justify slaughter in the name of humanity just as easily as god-believers can do so in the name of God. Its dogmatic treatment consists in giving it an existence of its own and in making it more important than ourselves. Extremists typically do this when they use notions such as God, life, freedom, or equality to justify maiming and murdering people. The beliefs have become more important than people who become means to the ends of ideology or religion rather then ends in themselves.

We can also keep our notion of humanity in perspective by entering such contexts as life, society, and the universe, as well as by taking account of other people's points of view. We use our judgment to interrelate all these perspectives rather than being stuck in one or other of them. We reconcile conflicting moral obligations by prioritizing them in relation to different contexts rather than confining them to one context alone. The uncertainties involved compel us constantly to apply our judgments flexibly and with sagacity rather than rely on absolute values that prevent us from thinking things out properly.

In contrast, there are no limits to any notion of God. It is presumed to apply everywhere and at all times. All thoughts and intuitions can be considered to be god-given. If the notion is treated self-referentially, it will always be used to justify the most extreme and evil of actions. Treating God self-referentially leads us to identify the notion with ourselves. As God has not manifested itself as an identifiable zoological species, it can't be referred to in nature except by reducing it to something else by way of metaphor, and this can only be humanity. If the notion of God means anything at all, it refers ultimately to ourselves, since we must draw on our own experiences of life and the universe to picture God. Any clear view of God can only be humanity writ large since God can only have humanly conceivable powers and abilities. Humanity might, for instance, become omniscient and omnipotent in the far future.

Thus, having faith in God must mean having faith in ourselves. The feeling of a divine presence implies only that we are sensitive to the possibility of our being seen by others who are currently unseen by us. In any case, speculation about the existence of any god or superior beings is now properly the province of science fiction rather than theology which assumes in advance the truth of that which it purports to prove, namely, that God exists, one way or another. Feature films and television programmes such as The Matrix, the Startrek and Stargate series provide us with more honest and imaginative insights into god-like capacities than theologians ever do. And such capacities are always explicable in broadly scientific terms. There is no need to give supernatural or divine explanations that are beyond all scientific understanding.

5. Our moral obligations

Strengthening the will and power within us to make the most of our lives and never be downhearted or defeated, is therefore humanism's ultimate aim. Religion does the opposite in sapping our inner strength in the name of external, supernatural entities to which we are to submit ourselves without further thought or question concerning their real existence.

Though the humanist is sceptical of heartfelt beliefs, he need not be crippled by indecision or frozen into inaction. He can use different perspectives and contexts to help him arrive at correct and decisive judgments concerning right and wrong. Thus, within the context of humanity, we have certain moral obligations. These are implied by the indisputable facts of our collective existence. For example, the future of humanity depends on enough babies being born to ensure our survival from one generation to the next. This biological fact implies that most men and women must marry to produce children and provide a stable family life for them. This is a measurable moral imperative dependent on population replacement ratios. Exceptions to the rule would have to be well founded. Excuses on grounds of immaturity or sexuality would not be admissible, as they do not preclude the fulfilment of one's biological function as a parent.

Such moral obligations depend not on external authority but on personal responsibility. They stem from our being human and belonging to the human race. Thus, being responsible adults means that we often feel ourselves obliged to conform whether we like it or not. But it is important that we conform because we want to and for our own reasons and not just because of external compulsions such as laws or social norms. By promoting such personal and social responsibility systematically through education and example, we would not need the increasingly overregulated and law-ridden society presently being foisted upon us.

6. Embracing what is valuable about religion

It is not good for us to have everything cut and dried and served to us on a plate. The humanist recognizes the uncertainties in life and the need to struggle and fight to get anywhere. Nothing lasting can be achieved without effort and willpower. But religion tends to cocoon people with pleasing doctrines to make life seem easier than it really is. It engenders complacency and mediocrity. A happy, clappy, cheery, chirpy attitude seems all very nice but it brings out the worst as well as the best in people. It polarizes humanity and encourages wolf-like extremists to prey on sheep-like innocents. In contrast, humanism offers hope for the future because it clarifies the middle road and deliberately eschews the extremes to which we are all too easily prone.

But even if the humanist disbelieves in or disapproves of religions in general, he has no wish to prevent anyone from exploring the insights to be found in religions. A great deal of knowledge about morality and the human condition can be learnt from studying them. He himself finds interest in them because he seeks enlightenment in all human thought. He believes in people's inner being though not in their religiosity. He scorns to believe in any one faith to the exclusion of all others. The faiths of the past should be studied with the future in mind and not adhered to indefinitely as everlasting truths.

As already stated, what the humanist objects to most in religion is the enforcement of belief by authoritarian organizations that require absolute belief in sacred scripture and expect total obedience to those in positions of power and authority as conditions for membership of the organization. He expects organizations to facilitate people in reaching their own beliefs rather than dictate those beliefs to them. Thus, authoritarian organizations that do people's thinking for them, may be superseded in time by humanist organizations that encourage people to think for themselves.

There is no reason, except that of authoritarian conformity, why Christians have to be nothing but Christians, Jews nothing but Jews, Buddhists nothing but Buddhists, and so on. Why can we not be Islamic Christians, Jewish Sikhs or whatever? It is not just the humanist view that we should partake of any religious beliefs which interest us. There was after all a comparative religion movement which was active up to the nineteen sixties (as was pointed in the previous paper on 'The Need to Complete the Secularization of Society'.) However, the movement seems to fallen victim to resurgent fundamentalism in all religions in recent years.

In summary, therefore, the humanist finds abiding interest in the content and intent of religion but he objects to two aspects that distinguish religion from humanism. These are, firstly, the absolute beliefs that may not be criticized, altered or improved and, secondly, the authoritarian organizations that use power and authority to intimidate people and do their thinking for them. Humanism does not threaten anyone's religious beliefs but only the imposition of these beliefs in an authoritarian manner to become rigid religions. Therefore, humanism offers a better future for humanity because humanistic toleration inhibits the use of power and authority to create religions based on absolute and unquestioned belief. People would no longer be divided against each other because of their religious beliefs. Minute distinctions between their beliefs would no longer be the source of arbitrary, sectarian conflicts. We must learn to believe for ourselves alone and not for everyone else. Universal belief is superseded by personal belief. When everyone's religious beliefs are held humanistically then humanism rules, and religion is extinct. Humanism is the future; religion is the past.

Concluding Remarks

This humanist faith suggests the possibility of a more edifying and rational alternative to religion. In 1860, Ralph Emerson envisioned the possibility of such an alternative in his masterly essay, *The Conduct of Life*, (in which he surveys all human life, good and bad):

> There will be a new church founded on moral science, at first cold and naked, a babe in a manger again, the algebra and mathematics of ethical law, the church of men to come, without shams, or psaltery, or sackbut; but it will have heaven and earth for its beams and rafters; science for symbol and illustration; it will fast enough gather beauty, music, picture, poetry.[8]

Humanist beliefs, such as those outlined above, could be the basis of such an alternative, after which its practical and institutional development becomes possible. New and more rational forms of ritual, ceremony and devotion may emerge that are more in keeping with today's society than with that of hundreds or thousands of years ago. It could grow out of the existing religions without neglecting or destroying their artistic, musical, literary, architectural, and other achievements. Humanity may be unified by a new orthodoxy based on humanist beliefs that transcends all religious beliefs without repressing them or eliminating them completely. We will learn to believe in things humanistically rather than religiously; open-mindedly rather than absolutely. Only humanism can give us real and rational hope for our future. The age of religion effectively ended by the middle of the 19th century when the physical sciences such as physics, chemistry and geology became completely free of theological, scriptural and clerical interference. The 21st century could see a new age of humanism emerging which embraces both science and religion in a new synthesis taking humanity forward to a more harmonious future. Time will tell.

Notes and References

1. Ralph W. Emerson, 'Representative Men', *Essays*, London: Collins (undated), p. 369.

2. Masculine personal pronouns are used here as these arguments are addressed particularly to men who often have more difficulty than women in adopting the humanist mindset.

3. William James, 'Is Life Worth Living?', last paragraph, in *The Will to Believe*, New York: Dover Publications, 1956, p. 62.

4. Richard Dawkins, *Unweaving the Rainbow*, London: Penguin, 1999, p.3.

5. Cf., for instance, Erich Fromm, *The Sane Society*, London: Routledge, & Kegan Paul, 1963. This is also the subject of an e-book of mine that emphasizes the need to *Punish the Person, not the Crime* if we are to eliminate the criminal mentality in our society.

6. The unnatural nature of national divisions was noted 250 years ago by Edmund Burke. See his *A Vindication of Natural Society*, (1756) in *Selected Writings and Speeches*, New York: Anchor Books, 1963, p. 51.

7. Cf. Richard Dawkins, *The Ancestors' Tale*, London: Orion Books, p. 416

8. R.W. Emerson, *Nature, The Conduct of Life*, Everyman, 1963, p. 268.

IV. A Humanist Answer to the Big Questions

We constantly hear about 'people of faith' and 'faith groups' as if not having a religion *ipso facto* means that one cannot have a faith of any kind. Humanists are often discriminated against because they allegedly don't belong to any such groups. But faith is not the prerogative of religion. Humanists can have beliefs as heart-felt as those of religionists. Perhaps we should be banging much more loudly on our own 'faith' drum. We should make it clear that we form the best 'faith group' of all because we are allowed to work our beliefs for ourselves. Religious faiths must be accepted on a take-it-or-leave-it basis – you either belong or you don't – whereas humanists can have any faith they like, or none at all, without anyone thinking any better or worse of them.

Because we don't have a religious faith, it is assumed that all our beliefs must be based on science and nothing else. This was brought home to me recently when I received a DVD from a religious person. It features an eloquent American preacher who poses the following questions as if only persons of faith could possibly answer them:

1. Who am I ?
2. What am I worth?
3. Where did I come from?
4. Why am I here?
5. Where am I going after I die?

The implication is that Christianity can answer these questions whereas humanists can't even pose them let alone answer them. It is assumed that humanists can only appeal to science for the answers and, as the questions have nothing to do with science, they must be unanswerable. On the contrary, humanism can clearly encompass beliefs that are not only heart-felt but also appeal to our reason because we can work it out for ourselves. The answers to these questions can also be worked out by each of us. It appears that humanists have the onerous task of teaching people that they can think for themselves so that it becomes second nature to them.

Here are the answers to the questions that occur to me though they are far from being definite answers. They are not intended to be religious dogmas. To my mind, they are more like intuitive hypotheses. Indeed I reserve the right to change these answers in the light of further thought, knowledge and experience.

Who am I?
This question can only be answered because I have self-identity. I am able to identify myself from everything else around me because of my language

abilities. These abilities come from my belonging to human society and they have no source outside that society. I find my identity as a human being within human society. The possibility of my being what I am is only possible because I am a product of the universe and a culmination of evolutionary development and of human cultural development. My merely existing as a human being makes me a representative of the whole human race. All humanity is written within me by my upbringing and education. The religious answer is that I get my identity from being created by God who made me in his image. This is an arrogant stance that absolves me from the need to do anything for myself since it is all God's doing whatever I do or fail to do. Humanism forces me to be responsible for myself while religion deprives me of personal responsibility. I am humbled before that task because it always seems to be beyond me. I am no longer inflated with my own importance by thinking myself to be made in God's image. I have the task of finding out what it is to be myself. Nothing in life is meant to be so easy that it does not involve obstacles and problems, whether surmountable or not.

What am I worth?
My worth depends not only on what I think of myself but also on what others think of me. I am worth what I do and accomplish in the world. My feelings and thoughts are worth something to me even if no one else is aware of them. My life has value because of what I feel about myself and of what others feel about me. Internally, my value lies in the purity and purposefulness of my feelings, thoughts and deeds. Externally, my value lies in my place and role in society. My existence also contributes to the sum-total of existences in the universe. The religious answer is that my worth resides in God and in committing myself to this entity. My value then depends on an abstraction which is not me and has nothing to do with me. If my worth has to depend on God then this devalues and degrades me since I am plainly nothing compared with God. Humanism is therefore much more about the true worth of human beings than any religion can claim to be.

Where do I come from?
I came from the natural processes of the universe that are responsible for all living beings. These processes produced life and ultimately the human race. My particular birth was made possible because of a relationship between my father and mother. From that relationship I emerged reluctantly but pugnaciously from my mother's womb in spite of all the odds against it. It is often said that we are children of universe as much as we are children of our parents. This knowledge makes me feel important in

spite of my insignificance in relation to the unimaginable vastness of the universe. As far as we know, nothing else in the universe can formulate answers to this question except intelligent beings such as ourselves, no matter how physically insignificant we are. To say that I come from God tells me nothing about what I am, whereas science gives me a very full answer about what is unique and valuable about me. Humanism therefore gives a much fuller answer to this question than any religion gives.

Why am I here?

As a living, purposeful organism, I am here to fulfil my potential as a human being. Being human consists in making the most of my life for the best possible reasons. Though I am here because of a remarkable chain of chance events, I can be thankful that I have been given this chance to do something with my life. It is a wonderful opportunity which I should cherish and exploit for the best possible reasons. Our very ability to pose the question 'Why am I here?' means that we can answer it however inadequate the answer may be. It is a perpetual challenge to us to find answers to that question that will make sense of our lives from our own point of view. This is more the role of philosophy than religion since philosophy encourages us to think for ourselves whereas religion gives us ready-made answers. Besides, a typical religious view would be that I am here because of the will of God and therefore I must serve God. But this assumes that I am capable of knowing the will of God in which case I identify myself with God in the act of understanding his will; just as I might identify myself with my boss in understanding what he or she expects me to do. But the difference is that I would be subjecting myself to the will of something which is alien, inhuman and ultimately unknowable. The motto of Clan Sinclair is 'Commit thy Work to God' but the only way I can make sense this, as a Sinclair, is that God in this context means 'humanity'. That way I serve something which is beyond me but at least understandable and reasonably concrete.

Where am I going after I die?

I don't need to go anywhere after I die. Humanism is wide open to speculations about what happens after we die, whereas religion excludes such open-mindedness in favour of fixed dogmas about reincarnation and the like. Science allows us to speculate to our heart's content whereas religion forbids speculation as being contrary to faith and scripture, and even as being blasphemous. Though my body dies and my personality ceases to exist, there is nothing in science to contradict the view that my life exists forever and can never be erased for the copybook of the universe. According to that view, all the events of my life are downloaded for perpetuity onto the fabric of the universe. Such is our ignorance of the nature of time that its passing from minute to minute could be a feature of the universe as a whole thus ensuring the indelibility of the passage of time for each of us. In other words, every event of our lives involves the universe as a whole and doesn't just disappear into oblivion like a fading memory.

Besides, I find it alarming to think that there may be a unknown future awaiting me after I die. It is easier to think that it all ends with death and this makes it incumbent on me to make the most of my life while I am privileged to have it. I don't need religious nonsense about reincarnation, rapturing or transmutation of the soul. I can have faith in the universe simply as it is without any superstitious trappings. Whereas religion only offers us imaginative fantasies about the after life, science explores real possibilities. We must stick with science because it offers the ultimate possibility of conquering death in a concrete manner. In the future, it may well be possible to download our respective personalities into the vacant brains of spanking new clones of ourselves. It is matter of finding out how to do this, and clearly neural science is heading in that direction. Unfortunately I will probably be long dead before that happens.

V. We are the Word

In the beginning was the Word, and the word was
with God, and the word was God.
John, ch. 1, verse 1.

The opening of John's gospel is utterly wrong, patently untrue and sadly mistaken. The word did not exist in the beginning since we, the human race, brought the word into being. How could words possibly exist without people being around to enunciate them? In the beginning there was nature, and nature was wordless. Nothing could be said about nature, either for or against it, until language existed to provide the words to do so. Only when we came along with our language skills, it became possible for something to exist that transcended nature, namely, our words concerning nature. We are both the product of nature and the maker of nature. We have arrived by natural processes and we can use words to make more of nature than what existed before. We do this not only with our scientific knowledge but also with our thoughts and speculations concerning life and nature.

Nature is no more than the natural processes and products of the universe as studied by science. However, our being able to study nature has made more of it than if we had never been around. We are able to say and do things in respect of it that never before existed in the universe. All our scientific knowledge is nature writ large. Everything that we do in the world is an expression of our natures, for good or for bad. Our words have given us the power to alter nature and to judge whether there is a real improvement or not as a result of our deeds.

Nature was made flesh in the word since 'nature' could not exist as a distinct notion until the word was invented by which we can refer to it. Indeed, without words in general, there can be no culture, civilisation or society. Without words, a painting is just a splurge of colour, a poem is blots of ink on a page, and a great speech is no more than buffets of sound on the ear. In short, words enable us to know ourselves and our place in nature. Great works of scripture depend on such words and they owe nothing to illiterate nature.

Words used to be sacred things with a life of their own. They were put into books that became holy objects of veneration. They were made out to be more important than human beings. The contents of these books became the inviolable word of divinity instead of the fallible work of equally fallible human beings. Now we can see words for what they are – a means of transcending our nature and of understanding our place in the universe. At first this was done through the fables of religion but more recently philosophy and science have given us a more satisfying and convincing view of things. We are not required to **believe** anything t hat philosophers and scientists tell us; instead we are challenged to **understand** their prognostications. In understanding philosophy in our own terms we are expanding our minds and relating ourselves more richly with the world we inhabit. Philosophy develops our minds whereas religion stunts their growth. This is the effect of absolute belief that ties down our thinking instead of expanding it. Our beliefs, such as they are, can now be based on our understanding of philosophy and science since they are based on reason, reality and evidence and not on revealed or absolute truths arrived at in ancient societies utterly alien to our own.

Nature has no more end or purpose than what is prescribed by the words of man. All the religions of the world have tried in their various ways to work out what life is all about and to proclaim their various messages accordingly. They have had their day as credible vehicles of ultimate truth. Our words expressing our beliefs about nature, life and the universe point to a new area of study – a logodoxia, perhaps. This would be neither a religion nor a science but include religious studies and the metaphysics of science. It is a way of embracing the messages of all religions without espousing any of them. By examining the links between humanity and nature, it can transcend what we are in physical terms and speculate about what we might or might not become in the future.

Eliciting our true nature is an endless task for us finite beings. We can never be certain about what else remains for us to know about ourselves. Religion simply precludes the inquiry by giving us preconceived answers to unanswerable questions. All these matters are perpetually puzzling and anything said in this area of study may be disputed and rethought *ad infinitum*. We will always entertain ourselves with speculations about nature, life, death, immortality, eternity, infinity, time, mind, matter, freewill, fate and what it is all about.

I look forward to the time when humanity has sufficient confidence in itself to convert its churches, chapels, cathedrals, temples, synagogues and mosques into **Disputariums** that discuss all the important questions about life and nature without answering any of them with total certitude. All the ministers, priests, rabbis, mullahs, ayatollahs and preachers in general can become qualified **disputants** who interact with their respective assemblages as equals in a sincere quest for truth and understanding. There would be no more need for priestly hierarchies or semi-autonomous religious organizations. We can still have moving ceremonies, rites and rituals, but let them be seen as life-enhancing rites of passage or as historical pageants and not as the obsessive expression of outmoded beliefs. Truly we have much to gain through the loss of religion.

Part Two

Dualism

VI. Supernaturalism and Naturalism

There are more things in heaven and earth, Horatio,
Than are dreamt of in your philosophy.
Shakespeare, *Hamlet*, Act I, Scene 5, lines 166-7.

In Shakespeare's play, poor old Horatio has trouble coping with Hamlet's apparent encounter with his father's ghost. Such encounters can only be imaginary in his view. There can be nothing supernatural really existing in the natural world. But it is argued here that such an extreme, absolute naturalism that confidently rules out the possibility of supernatural things and events is mistaken. It has too much confidence in the scientific view which itself is provisional and not absolute. In the long run, science is well capable of making sense of any phenomena that presently appears to be 'supernatural'. But in the short term, it needs to be open to explanations that do not conform to our current understanding of the laws of nature. To rule out dogmatically everything apparently 'supernatural' suggests a lack of imagination on the part of its adherents.

The problem is that it is by no means obvious what is or is not supernatural. What is natural is supposed to conform to natural laws and not to conflict with common sense and scientific knowledge. Yet there are many examples of phenomena that are not explicable by means of natural laws. To begin with, it is difficult to explain the power of mathematics to represent accurately the external world, especially by means of so-called 'imaginary numbers'. There are no mathematical principles or laws of physics that can explain how the square root of minus one can function meaningfully in mathematical equations or how it can have practical effects in the physical world. For example, electricians use it in dealing with electric circuitry. Yet it is a negative number that makes no sense as something existing in the real world. It might therefore be said to be supernatural since the laws of nature cannot explain its practical usefulness.

Moreover the whole of human culture cannot be explained in naturalist terms. Crowds of people watching men doing things with spherical objects on a rectangular patch of ground, or running round and round an elliptical track cannot be explained by the laws of nature; nor can they explain the power of music and works of art to move people. The beauty that we experience on seeing colourful objects is not accounted for by the physical nature of light waves reflected by the objects. Indeed, colours are said to be in our minds more that they are in nature. If they are not natural, are they therefore supernatural? Logic might encourage us to think so but the uncertainty is really results from the indefinite nature of what is or is not supernatural.

Physics is the ultimate science on which the naturalist's beliefs are founded. But some of the most recent speculations of physicists seem to border on the supernatural. Where in the natural world can we find evidence of the existence of the parallel universes, about which many physicists are so supremely confident? They can never be observed and no one can think of experiments that will reveal their existence to us. We can never perceive electrons but at least experiments constantly confirm their existence. Quantum phenomena are incomprehensible to us but theories based on their existence are outstandingly accurate and reliable. In contrast, parallel universes and the 'strings' of string theory are purely theoretical constructs whose existence is beyond experimental confirmation. Thus, physics itself verges on the supernatural in its speculations.

Such uncertainty about what is or is not supernatural seems to give succour to religionists who wish to be believe in a mystical relationship with God or any of the other absurdities of religion that provoke the naturalist to adopt his own extreme views. However, there is room for a moderate supernaturalist view that is based on science, common sense and a critical view of what can or cannot exist in the real world.

Clearly, the boundaries of the supernatural are by no means clear and a moderate supernaturalist will not be dogmatic about imposing them. Furthermore, it is argued here that the moderate supernaturalist is also a moderate naturalist and vice versa. Open-mindedness means that both positions interact with each other rather than oppose each other. A moderate naturalist will be open to the possibility that science cannot necessarily explain everything that occurs in the natural world. Some occurrences may be more than just coincidence or be beyond the ability of current science to explain them. On the other hand, the moderate supernaturalist will be open to the possibility that science can indeed explain all natural occurrences whatsoever.

It is arguable that there are more things in heaven and earth than extreme naturalists are prepared to countenance. This suggests the possibility of a moderate supernaturalist view that is also compatible with secularism. The various views may be summarized as follows:

The Extreme View	The Moderate View
Extreme naturalism is monist in its outlook. It has a single-minded view of nature. Everything that exists is included in the natural world and there is no possibility of anything existing outside it. Thus extreme naturalists will always argue against the possibility of anything existing or happening that cannot be explained in terms of physical laws or flaws in the person advocating such existents. Their minds are closed to the possibility of anything supernatural. They have only one answer to give and this makes them monists in their thinking.	**Moderate naturalism** is dualist in its outlook. It acknowledges the possibility of supernatural things and events but believes there can be a natural explanation for them if we look for the evidence or examine them closely enough. For instance, it is possible that our emotions are communicable over distance. Advances in science might find that our emotions tap into electro-magnetic or other energy forces. But until such speculations are substantiated, they remain in the realms of the supernatural. This encourages scientists to do research that will provide scientific explanations for such phenomena.
Extreme supernaturalism is the opposite from extreme naturalism. It involves believing in the absolute existence of gods, angels, ghosts, aliens and the like. It entertains the existence of magical forces, effects or influences which can undermine scientific endeavour. It is also monist as it takes a one-sided view that excludes science.	**Moderate supernaturalism** avoids such irrational extremes and encourages us to contemplate the existence of inexplicable phenomena that science cannot yet deal with. At the same time, it repudiates belief in the absolute existence of any supernatural existents or influences that may only be figments of our imagination. It also encourages scientific research.

The relationship between the various positions may further be pictured in this interactive quadrifoil ,matrix as follows:

Monist View	**Dualist View**	**Monist View**
	Moderate Naturalism	
	↕	
Extreme Naturalism ←	**Intuitive Interaction** →	Extreme Supernaturalism
	↕	
	Moderate Supernaturalism	

Beliefs concerning the natural world range in a spectrum from extreme naturalism to extreme supernaturalism. Moderate naturalism and moderate supernaturalism occupy the indefinite middle position wherein they interact with each other at the intuitive level. Intuition is important here because it allows us open-minded about new ways of thinking about things. The extreme views are monist and polarising; they veer away from each other and from the middle ground. The moderate views are dualist and they may be pictured not only by their interacting with each other in a straightforward manner. They can also be thought of as spiralling uniformly in relation to each other through time. If they spiral away from each other then they tend towards uncertainty that is resolved into monist views. If they spiral towards each other they reach one point which is monist and dogmatic. When we are open-minded in our thinking then our thinking is intuitive and we veer between extremes in a constant attempt to make up our minds, one way or the other. For the dualist thinker, the conclusions reached are never absolute or inviolable to criticism. They are always open to further consideration. This is essentially the humanist view as I argue in the next section on 'Dualism and Humanism'

Thus, moderate naturalism is identical with moderate supernaturalism but only **dualistically**; their identity is a function of their dualist interaction. They are not identical in a formal logical sense of being essentially or substantially the same thing. (This dualist form of logic is detailed in my forthcoming book on *Our Dualist Mentality.*) They are only identical in being brought into interactive relationship with each other. In so far as they interact with each other they form an organic process analogous to the way that the organs of our bodies interact with each other. These organs differ in themselves but are identical in their forming intimate interactive parts of the body. Without their continued interactive relationships, both the body and its organs cannot continue to exist.

Thus, in a sense we lose touch with the unity of our own thinking when we succumb to the one at the expense of the other and take either naturalism or supernaturalism to be the one and only answer. We are possessed by extremist, absolutist views and become blind to any other ways of thinking. They both have their contributions to make but we become close-minded and dogmatic when the naturalist view is allowed to rule out religious thinking altogether or supernaturalist view leads us to downgrade science as being untrue to the human spirit. Unless humanism embraces such moderate viewpoints, it has no answer to religion except a negative, polemical one that strengthens religionists in their prejudices instead of assuaging them.

VII. Dualism and Humanism

Abstract

It is argued in this paper that understanding dualism is essential to the future of humanism and to the future of humanity. The study of dualism consists in understanding the extremes of opinion and attitude to which we are all prone and which pervade every aspect of our society. These extremes are even today impeding our future and threatening to plunge the world into internecine struggles between factions competing for power and pre-eminence. The fruitless conflicts, wars and divisions caused by extremism will only be avoided when a dualist view is adopted that makes the 'either-for-us-or-against-us' mentality universally unacceptable. The dualist view can also help us to deal with situations that demand insight more than logic. A distinction is made here between naïve and systematic dualism in which the former refers to confused and muddled thinking whereas the latter involves organized and purposeful thinking to deal systematically with confusing and conflicting situations. There is also a spectrum between naïve dualism at one extreme and absolute monism at the other extreme. Most of us, most of the time, are systematic dualists subsisting somewhere in the middle. Our future is constantly threatened by those few people who have one answer to everything and are intolerant of any other answers. If the dualist view becomes prevalent they may learn to think differently. Humanism is distinct from religion in being essentially dualist in its outlook and in being prepared to countenance alternative views. The further development of the dualist view therefore strengthens humanism against its monist enemies who are looking for certainty and easy solutions.

Our essential duality

This paper is part of my campaign to promote dualism which is largely a neglected and despised topic.[1] It is important to clarify this topic from a humanist point of view because humanism is perpetually under threat from authoritarian solutions that are easier to grasp and simpler to implement than woolly humanist ones. The humanist view needs to be strengthened and it is argued here that a better understanding of dualism will contribute to this.

In this paper, I take the view that humanism is about human beings realising themselves in spite of all the difficulties and limitations of life. It concerns our humanness and what makes us distinct from animals. It rejects extreme views such as proclaiming the supremacy of the human race in any absolute or religious manner. It is about enabling people to make the best of their talents and abilities. This does not mean that we can behave in any way we like or live for ourselves alone. Such extreme views of humanism are monist views that are unworthy of it. Selfishness and self-centredness are no part of humanism in the best sense of the word. We need to strengthen the dualist view of humanism so that it can counter such extreme views of what it is about.

Dualism is about being interactive with our beliefs and opinions. We hold them at arm's length so that they do not possess us. It is about self-reference in which we refer back to our beliefs to criticize them. Monism on the other hand sees everything in terms of one thing which is thought to be the ultimate, absolute solution to complex problems. An obvious example of a monist solution is the view that capitalism is the one and only solution to all economic problems as opposed to any alternative that favours government intervention. Reality is not so simple that one 'ism' alone can encompass everything about it but monist thinkers consistently behave as their 'ism' can do so. Monist solutions to our problems are static, monolithic and inviolable to criticism. They are applied absolutely and without alteration so that they lead inevitably to dogmatic extremism in which the opposing view is demonized. If we interact dualistically with our views we can then deal with them objectively and do not take them to heart as being the ultimate solution.

Dualist interaction consists in one-to-one interactions in which an exchange between disparate processes produces something different. There is no logical equivalence between the one and the other because complex processes are involved, especially with regard to biological entities. Living processes are complexes of dualist interactions. They have their roots in chemical interactions such as that between sodium and chlorine producing an entirely different substance – salt.[2]

We are dualist beings because we are biological entities. We have internal workings that interact on a one-to-one basis with our external environment to keep us in harmony with it. We breathe in air and expel carbon dioxide. We imbibe food and water and expel liquid and matter accordingly. The metabolic processes inside us involve dualistic interactions that are markedly different from the activity in inorganic matter such as liquid and metal. As social beings we constantly interact with each other and with society and its institutions. Our thoughts are influenced by such interactions, and other people's thoughts are changed as a result of our interacting with them. What is inside us changes when we interrelate with what is outside us. This contrast between the internal and the external is inherently dualist.

Being merely human means that we are often in two minds about many matters. When we are all of one mind, we may be blinded to other ways of doing things and can harm ourselves, other life-forms and the planet in general because we are collectively stupid, as in the world-wide financial crisis from 2008 onwards. However, we are also a self-correcting species that realizes its mistakes and can do something about them. Humanity's activities are not unconscious or random like the swervings of bird flocks or the stampedes of animal herds. Our activities are constantly being observed, monitored and commented upon by self-appointed experts, journalists, pundits, academics and the like. By examining the consequences of our actions, we can rectify our mistakes, and this is done by interacting dualistically with our problems. As dualists, we do not expect to get everything right all at once but may hope to do so in the long run.

Single-minded persons often commit atrocities, like Nazi officers who plead that they are only following orders when they slaughter people mindlessly. Man's inhumanity to man often results from the voice of authority being pursued single-mindedly and inhumanely. Single-mindedness is fine in moderation and within reasonable limits. We often need it to get things done. But it is taken to extremes by absolute monists (as mentioned below) who know no limits in pursuing their ends. The dualist view draws attention to our limitations in that regard because it reminds us of the need to be self-critical. We can stop ourselves and think again and be less sure of our own reasonings. The interactive aspect of dualism reinforces this critical self-reference.

Because we are self-conscious beings, we are also self-corrective. We examine what we have done and correct ourselves when necessary. In interacting with ourselves, we figuratively loop back into our former thinking and correct it accordingly. The dualist view is therefore one of trial-and-error; a procedure that also underlies the scientific method and has ensured the remarkable success of science in transforming our society largely for the better. Dualist thinking therefore moves forward recursively in a dynamic and flexible way. It embraces opposing points of view instead of being stuck unyieldingly in one extreme viewpoint. This dynamic view is not completely realist or idealist, empiricist or rationalist, logical or intuitive. It embraces all of these in an interactive manner, that is to say, it moves from one viewpoint to the other and *vice versa*, according to what needs to be done in the real world in correcting imbalances, redressing injustices, and loosening rigid points of view.

We should regard opposing positions, such as left-wing and right-wing, empiricism and rationalism, as **dualist challenges** rather than irreconcilable paradoxes. These positions constantly challenge us to make sense of them and we live our lives confronting them and dealing with them. Perhaps the ultimate dualist challenge is to live as if one is going to live forever and also as if this is the last day of our lives. Resolving this paradox requires us to actively find the most important and lasting things to do, and the resolution demands our constant attention. If we regard it as nothing more than an irreconcilable paradox then we have no incentive to make anything of it. Thus, paradoxes should be regarded as dualist challenges to be overcome rather than dismissed because they are paradoxical.

As human beings we are both unique individuals distinct from society and collective units intimately involved in society. These incompatible positions must be constantly reconciled and this is best achieved when we are in our dualist frame of mind. As individuals we are not so unique that we can live entirely to ourselves. Extreme individuality makes no more sense than extreme conformity. We can learn to balance the two in a dualist manner. Our word 'idiot' comes from the ancient Greek word meaning those who live for themselves alone and do not participate in society at large. To make the most of ourselves we need to conform and find our rightful place in society. But this conformity is taken to extremes by those who obey authority single-mindedly. They are in a monist frame of mind and may lose their humanity by being in thrall to ideas, beliefs or opinions that are regarded as real and inviolable. They become pawns in the nefarious activities of the state or of some organisation whose activities are divorced from the interests of humanity as a whole.

We all have this problem of balancing individual self-expression with the social conformity that is needed to make the most of ourselves, and this balancing involves what is here called 'dualist interaction'. We interact with opposing ideas in a genuine effort to seek the best way forward instead of being stuck in the rut of one way of thinking. There is always another way of looking at things and this is the essence of open-mindedness.

We obey the law because we have good reason to do so but we always have the option of breaking the law if only because we are human and not mindless automatons. The dualist view recognizes the fragility of our humanity and is therefore the default position for human beings. Other animals may be driven by instinct and impulse but we always have the choice of doing or not doing what we feel like doing. This two-minded duality makes us dynamic and uncertain animals who are always trying to do things better in the future - every day being 'Groundhog Day'.

However, philosophers usually avoid this obvious duality in favour of a monist view of ourselves and the universe. The dualist view is too untidy and illogical, and their inclination is to reduce everything to one thing or idea. The truth is often conceived to be static, unyielding and eternal. But in the dualist view, truth is something we are constantly striving for by interacting with our environment. It is a process of continuous advancement and enlightenment rather than a fixed goal to be arrived at.

The fear of dualism

The dominance of formal, linear logic since the time of Aristotle has ensured that philosophers treat dualism with a mixture of fear and disdain. They associate it with equivocation and muddled, middle-of-the-road thinking. They have habitually rubbished it by one argument or another, but it will not go away. As mentioned above, living beings are essentially dualist, and our inner biological functions distinguish us from physical reality. These inner workings make us more than just lumps of matter. Our thoughts and feelings are often indefinite and neither one thing nor another. When we stop being dualist in our thinking, we go to extremes of one sort or another in search of absolute certainties. It is natural for us to have beliefs that we consider to be important, but absolute beliefs that are unqualified and held uncritically do us no credit. A dynamic, dualist view is required to make sense of our beliefs. Its previous fate is very briefly outlined as follows:

• Historically speaking, the dualist view was oversimplified in Descartes' mind/body distinction. It is much more complicated than a simple relationship between mind and body since the contents of mind and body are interacting dualistically within themselves. He viewed the mind as containing discrete substances rather than comprising processes that interact with what is distinct from it. In that more comprehensive view, the mind is as physical as everything else in the body.

• Kant might have arrived at it if he had not made the noumena inaccessible to human thought. We interact constantly with whatever we conceive to be real in order to stay in touch with reality. In that regard, we are alternately both 'transcendental idealists' and 'empirical realists', as we relate our ideas to reality and adjust them accordingly. Kant acknowledges this in many places in his first *Critique*, but his quest for linear, logical consistency leads him to make 'things in themselves' fundamentally inaccessible to us. He thought that we only have access to phenomena produced by categorization of our experiences. Therefore everything is in the mind, and we can only be 'transcendental idealists'. German idealism was the inevitable consequence of his view.

• Dualism was implied in Hegel's dialectic which was never developed beyond the simple triad of thesis, antithesis resulting in synthesis. The interaction is a logical one of assertion followed by contradiction resulting in a new, more unified assertion. The causal and cyclical nature of the interaction is never explored by him in any depth. In the end, he subsumes everything into his monist notion of the Absolute.

• More recent philosophers such as John Stuart Mill, William James, Henri Bergson and John Macmurray toyed with the dualist view but fought shy of adopting it wholesale. For example, William James recognized the dualist opposition between tough-minded and tender-minded thinkers in his seminal work, *Pragmatism*.[3] But his choice of the word 'tough' betrays his prejudice in favour of the former viewpoint. Indeed, his advocacy of 'radical empiricism' rules out rationalism and therefore falls short of being dualist.

• Borden Parker Bowne comes close to adopting a dualist view in his book, *Theory of Thought and Knowledge* (1899). He regards thought as "an organic activity which unfolds from within, and can never be put together mechanically from without." He makes interesting dualist contrasts such as 'theoretical impotence', 'practical impudence',nd 'theories of knowing'/ 'theories of being'. But he reduces the dynamism of his philosophy by grounding it on rigid categories such as time, space, number, quantity, quality, being, ideality and so on.[4] He thus follows the same Platonic path as A.N. Whitehead in his so-called 'process' philosophy that ties human thought down instead of liberating it.

•   The dominance of formal logic in the 20th century philosophy has ensured that the dualist view has been consistently dismissed out of hand. For instance, Gilbert Ryle's book, *The Concept of Mind* (1949), treats the 'inner' and 'outer' as no more than metaphors and 'the Ghost in the Machine' as a myth. More than metaphors and myths are involved in dualist thinking as it concerns what we do and how we behave. Also, our future depends on our having a realistic view of ourselves in which our inner construct conforms to outer reality by our interacting with our environment and not taking it for granted.

•   Karl Popper's 'Three Worlds' view implies a theory of dualist interaction in which there is interaction between the 'World 1' of physical reality and 'World 2' of subjective experience resulting in the 'World 3' containing our objective knowledge. However, he failed to develop the metaphysical implications of this dualist view to create a coherent system.[5]

•   Wittgenstein might have adopted a dualist view if he had not been such a monist thinker that he lurched from one extreme view to the other in his earlier and later philosophies. If he had been more dualist in his thinking he would have reconciled his disparate positions instead of taking two monolithic standpoints. He moved from a **logicism** in his *Tractatus* that proclaims the supremacy of logic to a **logomachy** that establishes the hegemony of language. In place of fixed, logical pictures, he offered endless, purposeless language games, thus stultifying philosophical discourse in both cases. The dualist view is required to liberate such stultification and take philosophy forward to new vistas.

•   The consequent dismissal of an inner life by behaviourists and others is manifestly mistaken because we all have thoughts and feelings that are never communicated with others. So far from arguing an inner life out of existence, we need to show its nature and make manifest the benefits of adopting it. In so doing, we can clarify many philosophical problems such as the self, mind, body, complexity and what is to be human. This would be a major contribution to our understanding of the human condition, and is at least a beginning and not an end in itself.

•   In conclusion, the philosophical study of dualism has failed to make progress because it has been too closely associated with Cartesian dualism. The spectre of Descartes has haunted the subject throughout the 20th century, spawning an ever-burgeoning and bewildering variety of distinctions and categories, both for and against dualism in this narrow Cartesian sense. Types of dualism include substance dualism, property dualism, predicate dualism, interactionism, parallelism, occasionalism, epiphenomenalism, non-reductive physicalism. One is expected to pick one or other of these positions and then argue for or against it. The only alternative is to invent yet more distinctions that add to the confusion instead of resolving it. For example, John Searle in an online paper entitled "Why I Am Not a Property Dualist", argues that his view is a "biological naturalism" rather than a 'property dualism'.[6] In contrast, the dualist view gets rid of the outmoded mind/body distinction altogether in favour of a complex web of dualist interactions that involve our relationship to the external world. All this is outlined in more detail in my forthcoming book on our dualist mentality.

Why humanism needs the dualist view

We can strengthen humanism against the criticisms of its opponents by stressing its dualist approach as opposed to a monist one. The latter seeks the comfort of absolute certainty by positing one view against all others as the one and only solution to all our problems. This certainty is usually found in religious fundamentalism or political ideology but may involve lifestyle obsessions with drink, drugs, food and the like. By incorporating the dualist view, humanism can make us secure within ourselves so that we can tolerate uncertainty and cease the vain pursuit for absolute certainty. By such means, we can learn to be content within ourselves while being dynamic in our relationships with our environment, society and life in general.

Both humanism and dualism are prone to extremes when they are applied as absolute solutions in themselves. Dualism is taken to extremes when a naïve, undiluted dualism leads to uncertainty, indecision, equivocation, and to relativist judgments by which any form of conduct may be justified. It is then akin to thoughtlessness as it lacks focus and direction. The remedy is a systematic dualism which is relentlessly interactive and dedicated to finding solutions, not by sitting on the fence but by viewing the situation as a whole and by taking account of opposing opinions on the matter, as is described below.

In the case of humanism, its extreme application may involve demanding the abolition of religion. This extreme view proclaims unequivocally the necessity for everyone to become atheists since there is no evidential basis for religion or the existence of God. But such extremism itself goes against humanism which surely deals with everything concerned with being human. When humanism is narrowed down to naturalism and atheism, this makes it sectarian and therefore not strictly humanist. Nothing is gained by the perpetual conflict caused by taking extreme stances. Tribalist loyalties are aroused which confound the interests of society as a whole. Militant atheism is counterproductive as it gives its opponents something to fight against. Established religions are regaining confidence and are becoming more focused because their existence is threatened unnecessarily by extreme views.

The dualist approach to religion is not to deprive people of it but to cater for the underlying need for it. It takes account of the inner life that is the source of religious feelings. This inner life includes our beliefs about the meaning and significance of our lives in the light of current knowledge. Local community centres can be created in which that inner life can be explored open-mindedly and without resorting to fixed doctrines imposed on people by a hierarchy of leaders who have privileged access to alleged 'truths'. (The role of such centres is outlined in my previous contribution to the EPH Journal, now section one in this book.)

Extreme humanists may also place excessive importance on left-wing, politically correct solutions and dismiss alternative views out of hand. They overlook the conservative view of things in favour of the liberal view. An interactive, systematic dualism will take account of opposing views such as the following:

Liberal	**Conservative**
Freedom	Security
Progress	Tradition
Nonconformity	Dependence
Self-Expression	Obedience

To avoid its own potential for extremism, humanism must be consciously dualist in its approach. This ensures its open-mindedness and tolerance which is reinforced by the dualist view. In so far as humanists are against prejudice, bigotry and narrow-mindedness, they must also be dualists. If we are not consciously dualist in our thinking then we are prone to go from one extreme to another. As Thomas Reid (1710-96) put it: "Extremes of all kinds ought to be avoided; yet men are prone to run into them; and, to shun one extreme, we often run into the contrary."[7] When Germany came under Nazi domination, many extreme left-wing people went to the other extreme and became ardent right-wing Nazis. A few members of the Nazi Party abhorred the extremes to which that regime took anti-semitism and other intolerances. Among them was Oscar Schindler who risked his life to help Jews as is justly celebrated in the outstanding feature film, *Schindler's List*. He was undoubtedly dualist in his thinking as he saw and appreciated the merits of the opposing view and acted accordingly.

The progressive and conservative modes of thinking have their basis in society in general. Some people seek change or support progress because they cannot stand the status quo. Others are against social change or progress in principle because of a fear or distrust of any change. These turns of mind may veer into two extremes: (1) an individualist way of thinking that supports debate, controversy, freedom and revolutionary change; (2) a communitarian way of thinking that cherishes law, order, security and good governance. The one is fundamentally non-conformist and the other fundamentally conformist:

SOCIOSPHERE
of communicable thought,
speech and action
↓
NONCONFORMIST
Liberal-Minded
Left-Wing
Freedom
INDIVIDUALISM

GOVERNANCE
of law, power, authority,
money and employment
↓
CONFORMIST
Conservative-Minded
Right-Wing
Security
PERSONHOOD

The Contrast Between Discursive Nonconformity and Methodical Conformity

The 20th century was characterized particularly by the wars and conflicts brought about by the fruitless and self-destructive opposition between right and left, fascist and communist and similar dichotomies. Even today there are senseless clashes between left and right wing groups such as between liberals and supremacists, anti-fascists and nationalists, and so on. If society as a whole cannot accommodate these extremes, it is hardly surprising that organizations within society are similarly plagued with such fruitless extremes of thinking that impede their progress. The dualist view is that we can take account of both extremes in our thinking.

We easily get into the mental rut of thinking along one of these lines of thought at the expense of the other. Either we become overconfident of our opinions or we have no confidence at all in them. Either we dismiss all opposition to our views out of hand or we accept mindlessly and uncritically the authority of tradition, gurus, demagogues, preachers or whatever. Instead of taking account of opposing views in an interactive way, we pit our views against the opposing ones and attempt to annihilate them. The result is party politics, warring factions, irreconcilable religions, and so on. In other words, our tribal and sectarian inclinations find their origin in such opposing grooves of thought. As a result, our prejudices are strengthened and they stultify our inner development.

Our hope for our future must lie in our learning not to lapse into the mental grooves that divide us from opposing points of view and prevent us from appreciating their value. For instance, from an educational point of view, students can perform mental exercises as part of civics courses in which they adopt opposing frames of thought and practice broadening their minds in that way. This is not learning to sit on fences but learning to think out the complexities involved in adopting any balanced and informed viewpoint.

The importance of the dualist view

The words 'dualism' and 'duality' are often used pejoratively to refer to contradictory and confusing behaviour: for example, the duality of behaving with sympathy at one moment and with hostility at the next moment. This is psychological inconsistency and no reflection on the notion of duality itself. The dualist view itself is thereby avoided so that it can dismissed without further examination. It is considered too indefinite and flawed to be seriously considered.

However, a better understanding of dualism is a mental tool that we can use to cope with conflict and uncertainty in our daily lives. Conflicting opinions are a necessary dynamic which can make or break an organisation. When people take sides and regard their opinions are more certain and truthful than those of the opposing side, the dualist view helps us to resolve the matter one way or the other. It may be uncertain as to which side is correct, beneficial, or whatever, but dualist thinking is about dealing with uncertainty rather than shying away from it.

Uncertainty is a necessary aspect of the human condition. Life would be boring if everything is predictable and reliable. If the outcome of a football game is certain beyond doubt, there would little point in paying to watch it. A football team that could win all its matches without fail would be promoted to a league of its own.[8] Similarly, there would be no need for leaders, politicians or managers if every situation pans out predictably and there are no doubts about how to deal with it. Computers and other machines are used when routines, processes and procedures can be worked out mechanically or algorithmically. When machines can deal with unpredictable situations as we do all the time, they will be the equal of us. (Turing's test is not rigorous enough to determine when computers are truly indistinguishable from human beings. The computer would show itself capable of thinking and feeling for itself without referring to anything else and thus evince unique and original thinking or imagination such that writers and artists daily display.[9])

Whatever is discrete and measurable can be analysed by logic and mathematics. But when we think ahead and make choices between alternatives, the process is often intuitive and qualitative. Decisions made on logical grounds can be as extreme as those made by intuition. If the bankers had thought dualistically instead of logically they might have recognized the extremes to which their behaviour was tending. The bankers' and financiers' activities before the credit crunch in 2008 were doubtless backed up by a whole array of reasonable arguments. The fact is that they were too rational and failed to think outside the box. It was not so much collective insanity that led to the credit crunch as too much trust in the rationality of their actions. Only a leader imbued with a flexible, dualist outlook could have broken the mould and shown them that they were going to absurd extremes in their reasonings. Obviously such a leader never emerged at the right time.

Success in life is often a black-and-white matter. Either we are successful at getting the job done or we are not – as a matter of fact. But how that success is achieved is not so clear-cut. In practical terms, we are concerned here with the means by which we may or may not achieve success through dualist thinking. A successful person is usually not just a lucky person but also one who takes account of both sides of any argument and also of the extremes to which each side may be taken by those who are prone to such extremes. In that way, they are able to take a balanced view of any situation and make realistic decisions which bear fruit.

The dualist view does not make us any the less decisive in our actions. Indeed, it gives a rational basis for decisiveness. Systematic dualism (as discussed below) considers the extremes to which our thinking can go. By so doing, it clarifies situations by revealing imbalances, imperfections, injustices, bottlenecks, and distortions which can be addressed and rectified. It clearly shows the direction in which action must be taken to achieve harmony, redress imbalances, perfect imperfections, remedy injustices, and relieve bottlenecks and distortions. For example, one can only hope to avoid taking an extreme view in politics by carefully considering the opposing view and evaluating its merits in a dualist fashion. The resulting view should be more balanced and enable one to act more justly having taken account of all factors involved in the situation.

Dualism is part of the human condition as we are alternately active and passive beings. It is in our nature to alternate between asserting ourselves boldly and retracting into our respective shells when things go wrong as a result. The history of philosophy may be viewed dualistically as an oscillation between dogmatism and scepticism, between the confident assertion of belief and the diffident doubt of it.[10] Evidently, philosophy is presently undergoing a sceptical phase. Perhaps it is now time for some dogmatic dualism to help us control our obsessions so that they do not control us. Our interests are a part of our life and not the be-all and end-all of life. The dualist view helps us to keep them in their place. We learn to externalize them by interacting with them dualistically. Conflicts can then be considered objectively to ensure that we deal with them in a balanced and systematic way.

However, the dualistic view is not simply about moderation in all things. It is about recognising the complications involved in a situation and, if necessary, going to opposite extremes to rectify an imbalance. For example, the prevalence of intolerance in some sectors of the community may itself be intolerable and require extreme measures to rectify it, as Karl Popper recognized in his 'Principle of Toleration'.[11] We cannot tolerate all forms of behaviour without question as is implied by extreme multiculturalism. A limit to tolerable behaviour must be set in the interests of social harmony. Another example is Aristotle's 'golden mean' between two extremes.[12] This is a static and artificial division that does not reflect the complexity of the real world. Thus, thinking of courage as a mid-point between rashness and cowardice is of no help in practical situations where something must be done or not be done, as the case may be. The courageous person does not deliberate between two extremes but acts intuitively because something must be done. Intelligent decisiveness comes from taking account all the circumstances involved in a situation. Thus, seeking a fixed balance between two extremes is naïve dualism if it does not result from a systematic view of the whole and of all the possibilities, as is argued below.

Avoiding the muddled middle

In Charles Dickens' novel, *Hard Times*, there is a character called Stephen Blackpool whose catchphrase is "'tis aw a muddle". He is a mill worker in the industrial north of England who cannot bring himself either to side with his fellow employees in their dispute with the mill owners or to take the protection offered by the latter. The employees wish to change their working conditions for the better whereas the employers want to preserve the status quo and protect their company's profitability and position in the market. The employees take a progressive view and the employers a conservative one. Blackpool sees the merits of both sides and refuses to identify with one extreme or the other. Inevitably, he is despised and shunned by both sides and leaves the town. When he is falsely accused of a bank robbery, he returns to the town to clear his name but falls down a mineshaft on his way there. Eventually he is found and in his dying words says it is a muddle from first to last. If things hadn't been so muddled, he wouldn't have needed to come back. If the workers hadn't been in a muddle among themselves, they wouldn't have misunderstood him, and so on.[13]

Stephen Blackpool is one of Dickens' many exaggerated characters who nevertheless give us an insight into the human condition. We can interpret him as a naïve dualist who is mired in the muddled middle. He sees that the truth is never as black and white as the clear thinkers make it out to be. The truth lies within the two extremes and it is easier to take sides than work out what should be done. The problem is to maintain a dualist view while avoiding uncertainty and indecision. Blackpool lacks the mental equipment to see his way forward, and therefore everything seems incorrigibly muddled to him. In short, he sits uncomfortably on the fence because he is not a systematic dualist who understands the nature of his position and is confident of its superiority over the extreme positions which it abhors.

The systematic dualist recognizes that there are only two clear responses to a confusing situation in which people take sides against each other. One can join one side or the other or one can work towards a resolution, reconciliation or synthesis which will take the situation forward and make progress possible. Taking the first alternative, the systematic dualist would join one side or the other and work hard to moderate the views of that side and achieve a reconciliation of some kind. Taking the second alternative, he or she would be confident enough to persuade both sides that conflict and confrontation cannot achieve their ends. In Blackpool's case, the first alternative is more likely to be successful than the second one, given the passions of both sides in such 19th century conditions. However, Blackpool clearly lacked the leadership qualities required to take the dynamic and purposeful action that the situation demanded. It is arguable that successful leadership depends on the use of systematic dualism to a greater or lesser extent.

Dualism is often associated with shiftiness, prevarication, hypocrisy and even immorality. But systematic dualists by virtue of being systematic in their thinking are also being consistent, reliable and moral in their behaviour. They are no longer being systematic when their behaviour lacks integrity. If they acquire the depth in philosophy that systematic dualism demands then they are more in touch with themselves and are less inclined to misbehave. Their conduct can be consistent with the highest standards of honour and respectability though being human means that they may fall from grace as readily as anyone. The recent lapses of the golfer, Tiger Woods, come to mind in that regard. Sooner or later, insincere, immature or malign personalities reveal their inadequacies as they are deficient in the self-criticism that the dualist view demands.   They no longer see themselves as others see them and are therefore incapable of behaving themselves.

The relationship of dualism to monism

For the dualist there are no fixed either/or, black/white alternatives as far as our beliefs and opinions are concerned. Both alternatives are always up for consideration. Thus, the systematic dualist never excludes entirely any opposing view, even the monist view. Monism in this context is a single-minded and exclusive devotion to ideas, ways of thinking, ideas, hobbies, lifestyles, and so on. Monism is not an absolute alternative to dualism as it has its place in human affairs just as dualism has, and indeed it forms part of the dualist view. There is a spectrum between monist and dualist attitudes and we are all monists and dualists to some degree or other. But we must never lose touch with our inner dualist and become absolute or extreme monists.

Absolute monists who give no credence to opposing views can be a menace to society, especially when they know no bounds to their fanaticism and enthusiasm. Terrorists, extremists and hot-headed fanatics are typically absolutist in their thinking. Less extreme monists are simply bores when they systematically interpret everything in relation to one thing. These include those whom the essayist William Hazlitt graphically describes as 'people with one idea.'[14] Having one idea means that every conversation is brought round to it as if it were *sine qua non* of their existence.

However, we are all moderate monists in our everyday pre-occupations with hobbies, football teams, shopping or whatever grabs and interests us most in life. Moderate monists are amateur enthusiasts who are fanatical about their interests but only within limits. Their interests are always balanced by other interests and responsibilities such as earning a living, pursuing a career, raising a family, political activity and so on. We can therefore distinguish absolute, extreme and moderate monists along a spectrum that includes the dualist view at its moderate end.

In our daily lives we can be both moderate monists and systematic dualists. The latter means being moderate in our prejudices and pre-occupations, and the former means recognizing the alternatives that are always possible. We must judge when to be carefully doubtful and when to be cautiously certain. Great and successful leaders are usually adept in combining moderate monism with systematic dualism in being flexible and creative in their thinking and behaviour while also being certain and surefooted in their decision-making. The full spectrum between monism and dualism may be represented as follows:

Absolute Monists — Extreme Monists — **Moderate Monists/**
Systematic Dualists — Naïve Dualists — Absolute Dualists

The spectrum ranges from absolute clarity to absolute obscurity as absolute monists have absolutely no doubt about their beliefs as much as absolute dualists doubt everything as a matter of policy. Absolute dualists are true sceptics and even apply their scepticism single-mindedly so that paradoxically they are absolutely monistic in that regard. The same kind of paradox arises when dogmatic left wingers become fascists in enforcing their views, or when extremely conservative people are notoriously lax and permissive in their moral behaviour. In other words, absolutists end up chasing their tails and confirming that which they deny. These distinctions are summarised as follows:

- **Absolute Monists** despise moderation and give no credence to opposing views. They know no bounds to their fanaticism and enthusiasm and are often a menace to society. Terrorists, extremists and hot-headed fanatics are typically absolutist in their thinking. In absolute dualism, the world is divided absolutely into black and white, good and evil, matter and spirit, mind and body and so on. The thinking of absolute monists is dominated by categorical thinking in which the world is dividing into rigid categories. You are either for them or against them.

- **Extreme Monists** systematically interpret everything in relation to one thing without using violence to enforce their views. Having one idea means that every conversation is brought round to it as if it were *sine qua non* of their existence. To be obsessed about one's hobbies, about losing weight or about any number of such fixations is to be an extreme monist.

- **Moderate Monists** – This is what we all are in our everyday pre-occupations with hobbies, football teams, shopping or whatever grabs and interests us most in life. As moderate monists we are amateur enthusiasts who are fanatical about our interests but only within limits. Such interests are always balanced by other interests and responsibilities such as earning a living, pursuing a career, raising a family, political activity and so on. But moderate monists are also systematic dualists by the very fact of being moderate in their monist indulgences.

- **Systematic Dualists** recognise when faced with opposing sides that there are only two clear responses to a confusing situation in which people take sides against each other. One can join one side or the other or one can work towards a resolution, reconciliation or synthesis which will take the situation forward and make progress possible. Taking the first alternative, the systematic dualist would join one side or the other and work hard to moderate the views of that side and achieve a reconciliation of some kind. Taking the second alternative, he or she would be confident enough to persuade both sides that conflict and confrontation cannot achieve their ends.

- **Naïve Dualists** are without any systematic approach by which to cope with their dualist views. They have the muddle-headed, fence-sitting kind of dualism in which one is unable to make up one's mind. They are like Buridan's ass that had equal piles of hay on either side of it. As it was unable to make up its mind which pile to eat, it starved to death. Such dualists clearly lack the internal *nous* and the leadership qualities required to take the dynamic and purposeful action that the situation demands.

- **Absolute Dualists** divide the world absolutely into good and evil, matter and spirit, mind and body and so on. The Manicheans were absolute dualists as was Descartes with his mind/body dualism which lacked a coherent interaction between these extremes. These views are also absolute in that they interpret the world by means of only one form of dualism to the exclusion of all others. Like all absolutists you are either for them or against them.

In everyday life, we can be both moderate monists and systematic dualists. We incorporate both ways of thinking without being aware of it. The latter means being moderate in our prejudices and pre-occupations, and the former means recognising the alternatives that are always possible. We must judge when to be carefully doubtful and when to be cautiously certain.   Great and successful leaders are usually adept in combining moderate monism with systematic dualism. They are invariably flexible and creative in their thinking and behaviour while also being certain and sure-footed in their decision-making. An outstanding example of this is Oliver Cromwell whose conversation could be baffling and hard to understand but whose actions and battle strategy were decisive and effective.[15] This duality is often called 'common sense' but dualist theory goes much further than Thomas Reid and the Scottish Common Sense School in elucidating what it is.

We can all identify with Robert Graves' poem, "In Broken Images".[16] We are "slow, thinking in broken images", while others are "quick, thinking in clear images." We reach a new understanding of our confusion while others experience a new confusion of their understanding. The systematic dualist view is that clarity resides with facts, things and events while confusion and uncertainty may justly reign in our views, opinions, beliefs, convictions which are peculiar to ourselves. Formal, linear logic is needed for the former but a dualist, dynamic logic is required for the latter. We may be certain, reasonable and logical about facts that we all share but we often have to suspend judgment about our own opinions. A different logic is required in which the middle view is not excluded. We must be more inclusive in our thinking. Being open-minded and forward thinking means that we hold our opinions at arm's length and with some doubt and uncertainty. In contrast, the absolute monist errs in attributing absolute truth and clarity to his or her beliefs and in attempting to eliminate doubt in matters in which doubt is more often a virtue than a hindrance.

The Coalition government formed in the UK between the Conservatives and the Liberals is an example of the dualist view at work. It was a coalition of two political parties that have their origin the 17th century Civil War between the Cavaliers supporting the King, and the Roundheads supporting parliament. Following the 1660 Restoration, the Court and Country parties in parliament became the Tories and the Whigs which in turn became the Conservative and Liberal parties in the 19th century. If the ethos of this coalition survives, it might mark an end to the absolute division between conservative and liberal minded persons. The lack of clarity introduced by this Coalition is perhaps inevitable since the avoidance of authoritarian rule depends on politicians not having everything their own way. It is always the case that "much might be said on both sides"[17] and the fact is that an open, translucent political system depends on both sides getting a hearing.

In daily life, however, it is often necessary to be decisive and surefooted. Systematic dualists must necessarily hone their judgments to ensure that decisive action is taken when required. They will thrive on oppositions and the pleasure of reconciling them to achieve worthy ends which are otherwise defeated by the acrimony aroused by such oppositions. They will seek unity and unanimity in relation to the aims of society. Effective leadership can always inspire and motivate people so that they fight for common causes rather than against each other. But it is successful only when it eschews the extremes and shows clearly the benefits of the middle way. When left wingers and right wingers make enemies of each other then the middle way is lost and society can lose its sense of direction. This loss is exemplified all too clearly in the next part of this book.

The middle way represented by systematic dualism is essential for creativity as it depends on our maintaining a balance between thinking too much or too little. It is arguable that those 'geniuses' who perform extraordinary feats of creativity are only able to do so because they are systematic dualists who avoid self-defeating extremes in their thinking. They develop their mental powers in a purposeful fashion without taking themselves too seriously on the one hand or belittling themselves too much on the other hand. Often we are in doubt whether to think too much of ourselves or too little. Here are the extreme consequences of the opposing tendencies involved:

<table>
<tr><td align="center">Thinking too much of oneself
may lead to</td><td align="center">Thinking too little of oneself
may lead to</td></tr>
<tr><td align="center">Hot-headed extremism
involving</td><td align="center">Empty-headed indifference
Involving</td></tr>
<tr><td align="center">Brazen overconfidence
and in extremis to</td><td align="center">Insipid lack of confidence
and in extremis to</td></tr>
<tr><td align="center">Homocidal sociopathy</td><td align="center">Suicidal self-abnegation</td></tr>
</table>

It appears that too many young people are prone to these extremes these days, leading to an outbreak of massacres and suicides, as reported by the mass media. Suicide bombers seem to incorporate both these strands in their thinking. Their unbalanced thinking twists these strands into a deadly double helix, the antithesis of DNA which gives life instead of taking it. A rational dualist interaction between these extremes is required to avoid being possessed by them beyond sense and reality. Thus, a greater understanding of our essential duality is the next great step forward for humanism and humanity.

Notes and References

1. Several passages of this paper originate, mostly revised and rewritten, from my paper, 'The Role of Dualist Thinking in Management', read to the Philosophy of Management Conference

at St. Anne's College, Oxford on 23rd July 2010. (See www.managementphilosophers.com *Accessed 2012-09-01*)

2. The nature of dualist interaction and self-reference is dealt with in more detail in my book on *The Promise of Dualism*.

3. William James (1907), *Pragmatism*, Cambridge: Harvard University Press, 1975, Lecture One, p.13.

4. Borden Parker Bowne, Theory of Thought and Knowledge, New York and London: Harper & Brothers Publishers, 1899. Preface, pp. iii; v; Introduction, p.4; and Ch. IV, The Categories.

5. Cf. Karl Popper (1972), Objective Knowledge, Oxford: OUP, 1975, ch. 3, p. 106f and ch. 4, p. 153f.

6. John R. Searle (1983), "Why I Am Not a Property Dualist", available at:
    http://ist-socrates.berkeley.edu/~jsearle/132/PropertydualismFNL.doc *Accessed 2012-09-01*

7. Thomas Reid, Essays on the Active Powers of the Human Mind, as in Sir William Hamilton's edition of The Works of Thomas Reid D.D. (Edinburgh 1895 - also Georg Ohms 1983), p. 635b.

8. Perhaps such an outstanding team might become an exhibition team that tours the world, like the basketball team, the Harlem Globetrotters, its members becoming celebrities in their own right. However, competitive sport usually involves an element of uncertainty and unpredictability to attract spectators and partisans.

9. A. M. Turing, "Computing Machinery and Intelligence," *Mind*, 1950, Vol. LIX, No. 236. This famous paper is excerpted in Hofstadter and Dennett's book, *Mind's I*, Penguin Books, 1982, pp.53-68. The question of whether a machine is thinking or not may be resolved by observing how it is behaving to itself rather than to people, as Turing suggested. Its inner life, consciousness and self-identity will consist in its having feelings, thoughts and ideas of its own. We will react emotionally to their displays of emotion and will either empathize or not as the case may be. As with human beings, what they are actually feeling may be uncertain even to themselves.

10. This dualist view of the history of philosophy is outlined in my book, *What is Philosophy?* Edinburgh: Dunedin Academic Press, 2008.

11. Cf. Karl Popper, *The Open Society and its Enemies*, (1945), London: RKP, 1969, Vol. I, Ch. 7, Note 4, p. 265.

12. Aristotle, *Nicomachean Ethics*, Book Two, Section 7, 1107a28. See Penguin edition (1987) p. 104.

13. Charles Dickens, *Hard Times*, 1854, New York: New American Library, 1961, Bk. III, Ch. VI, pp. 267-8.

14. William Hazlitt, 'On People With One Idea', *Table Talk*, 1824, London: J. M. Dent, 1908, Essay VII, pp. 59-69.

15. Cf. Sir Walter Scott's extraordinary portrayal of Oliver Cromwell in his novel, *Woodstock*. It seems convincingly true to life.

16. Robert Graves' poem 'In Broken Images' is freely available online.

17. Joseph Addison (1672-1719), in his Roger de Coverely essays in *The Spectator*, no.122, July 20, 1711. See also no. 117, July 14, 1711: "There are some Opinions in which a Man should stand Neuter, without engaging his Assent to one side or the other. Such a hovering Faith as this, which refuses to settle upon any Determination, is absolutely necessary to a Mind that is careful to avoid Errors and Prepossessions."

VIII. World War One and the Loss of The Humanist Consensus

Abstract

European civilization largely lost its sense of direction after World War One when its humanist consensus, that promoted human betterment, collapsed into a fruitless political opposition between left and right wing extremism. This collapse is here exemplified by the breakdown in relationship between left winger Bertrand Russell and right winger D.H. Lawrence during WW1. However, the real causes of the loss of the humanist consensus are more deep-rooted, as that consensus has its roots in the Renaissance and Enlightenment movements when the influence of humanist views was at its height. By the late 19th century imperialism and militarism threatened the consensus, and the senseless slaughter of WW1 brought it to an end. The humanist consensus re-emerged post-WW2, largely through American influence, but it has declined since. To restore the consensus, it is argued here that humanism can be strengthened by dualist theory and by a process of contextualization that brings humanity to the fore. By using 'connecting contexts' we can open our minds to larger perspectives. In that way, we are collectively more inclined to be optimistic about our prospects. The future of humanity seems to depend on such developments in our critical thinking about ourselves.

Introductory

Following World War One (WW1), Europe lost the great impetus of civilization which was taking it forward to an ever better future. That impetus was already petering out due to the causes that also brought about that cataclysmic war. Also, the USA was already poised to take over the mantle of civilized progress from Europe. The effect of the war was to end decisively the humanist consensus in Europe that was needed to maintain an optimistic view of its future and to continue cohesive progress on all fronts. This consensus had consisted in an overall belief in (1) the ability of individuals to better themselves and (2) the ability of humankind to better itself and make a better future for itself. The consensus was a general agreement that formed the spirit of the times. It engendered optimism and a faith in humanity that transcended religious belief. Its loss resulted in a polarization of politics between the left and the right. Radically minded people began to think of themselves as having nothing in common with conservatively minded people, and *vice versa*.

Pre-WW1, there was an air of optimism throughout Europe that contrasts with the general pessimism of today. Nowadays, every disaster or setback anywhere in the world is amplified by the mass media into harbingers of the doom awaiting us. The consensus today favours the revival of religion as being our only hope for the future. Thus, humanism's future depends on our restoring faith in humanity's ability to cope with the future and whatever it throws at us. It is argued here that the restoration of this faith depends on our modifying the social, political and religious extremes which will otherwise rend our society apart. A renewed humanist consensus is required to unify the world and take us all forward to better times.

When the humanist consensus was lost after WW1, European civilization lost its sense of direction, and the extremes in politics began to dominate. The authoritarian ideologies of communism and fascism swirled into the vacuum left by the absence of a dominant humanist consensus. Immediately after the war, Lenin and Mussolini rose up and were followed by Stalin and Hitler. Even in the UK and France, passionate persons devoted themselves to promoting these ideologies as if they were absolute truths thus alienating more thoughtful and open-minded persons. The story is somewhat different in the USA where the humanist consensus, enshrined in the American Dream, has been more predominant, at least until the last few decades during which religion and god-belief have resurfaced in a significant way.

It is argued in this paper that the humanist consensus, promoting the future betterment of humanity, involves a connecting interaction between the left and right wings in politics. Humanism at its most open-minded involves such an interaction, and its future depends on its maintaining a dualist view embracing these two outlooks, (as I have argued previously in the paper, 'Dualism and Humanism', reproduced here as section seven above.) When there is no longer a consensus between left and right, they become alienated from each other and regard each other as being the principal obstacle to future progress. They go to extremes in their indictment of each other: the left considers the right to be doctrinaire, cruel and oppressive; the right looks on the left as being sentimental, self-indulgent and decadent. The one then strives to eliminate the other, and the stage is set for self-sustaining internecine conflicts bringing no progress and only misery to humanity.

In this paper, the loss of humanist consensus after WW1 is illustrated by the fall-out between Bertrand Russell, the left wing philosopher, and D.H. Lawrence, the right wing novelist.[1] It was a pivotal moment in European history. The rest of the paper discusses the problem of restoring the humanist consensus and thus renewing people's confidence in humanity's future. It is suggested that a dualist view of the role of contexts in our thinking will help people to take the larger view of things. To understand our proper place in the scheme of things, it is necessary to enter the larger contexts of humanity and futurity for example.

Russell and Lawrence

The post-WW1 loss of humanist consensus is nowhere shown more strikingly than in the break-up of the relationship between Russell and

Lawrence. This break-up occurred during the winter of 1915-16, and Lawrence described how things fell apart in the following passage:

> It was in 1915 the old world ended. In the winter 1915-1916 the spirit of the old London collapsed; the city, in some way, perished from being a heart of the world, and became a vortex of broken passions, lusts, hopes, fears, and horrors. The integrity of London collapsed, and the genuine debasement began, the unspeakable baseness of the press and the public voice, the reign of that bloated ignominy, *John Bull*.[2]

Lawrence was partly expressing his bitterness at the treatment of his novel, *The Rainbow*, which had been prosecuted for obscenity in 1915; hence his contempt for 'John Bull' and prejudiced public opinion. But he was also disillusioned in his attempt to engage with the English intellectuals and inspire a revolution in their thinking. They included John Maynard Keynes, Lytton Strachey and the rest of Bloomsbury set.[3] In particular, he collaborated for a time with Bertrand Russell. They met for the first time in February 1915 at the behest of Ottoline Morrell. At the time they thought that together they could change with world for the better. They discussed the organization of joint lectures. Lawrence would deliver lectures on a religious theme and Russell on ethics and politics.[4] Russell expressed his initial feelings about Lawrence in this way:

> I liked Lawrence's fire, I liked the energy and passion of his feelings, I liked his belief that something very fundamental was needed to put the world right. I agreed with him in thinking that politics could not be divorced from individual psychology. I felt him to be a man of certain imaginative genius, and, at first, when I felt inclined to disagree with him. I thought that perhaps his insight into human nature was deeper than mine. It was only gradually that I came to feel him a positive force for evil and that he came to have the same feeling about me.[5]

Subsequently, Russell realized that they differed from each other more than either of them differed from the Kaiser of Germany. He also believed that Lawrence was espousing fascism before politicians such as Mussolini and Hitler got around to it.[6] Significantly, it was through their correspondence concerning the proposed lecture course that they gradually fell out with each other. Russell went on to deliver the lectures himself and they were published in the book, *Principles of Social Reconstruction* (1916).

The estrangement of Russell and Lawrence was not repaired by any subsequent correspondence; any more than the letters between Freud and Jung or between Rousseau and Hume could have renewed their respective friendships. Correspondence by letter is not an effective way to sustain an intellectual relationship between people with strong views, both of whom believe they are on the right track. They move away from each other with each written expression of opinion which is read from an unsympathetic point of view. They fall into mutual acrimony as they see more and more faults in the other's expressed opinions.

Though Russell demonized Lawrence till the end of his life, Lawrence avoided the fascist extremes of which Russell accused him. While he sometimes displayed a middle-class kind of anti-Semitism common at the time, he joined no fascist political party, nor would he have condoned Nazism. He seems not to have mentioned Hitler in his writings. As he died in 1930, he probably did not anticipate Hitler's rise. When Lawrence spoke of 'blood knowledge' he wished to bring it into balance with the intellect, while the Nazis sought to eliminate the intellect altogether.[7] Indeed, he abhorred the bullying tactics of both communists and fascists. When he came across gangs of young political extremists in Germany in February 1924, he saw them as throwbacks to a primitive tribalism.[8] He would likely have seen Nazism in the same light. The critic, Terry Eagleton places Lawrence on the radical right wing, as being hostile to democracy, liberalism, socialism, and egalitarianism, though never actually embracing fascism.[9]

In his writings, Lawrence often expresses humanist views. Some of what he says in his last book, *Apocalypse*, rivals Dawkins at his most lyrical:

> What man most passionately wants is his living wholeness and his living unison, not his own isolate salvation of his 'soul'. Man wants his physical fulfilment first and foremost, since now, once and once only, he is in the flesh and potent. For man, the vast marvel is to be alive. For man, as for flower and beast and bird, the supreme triumph is to be most vividly, most perfectly alive.[10]

Lawrence may be culpable for his radical right wing stance, but he did not condemn Russell to the extent that the latter condemned him. He resorted to no more than ridicule when a friend told him that Russell had said: "Lawrence has no mind". Lawrence replied: "Have you seen him in a swimsuit? Poor Bertie Russell! He is all Disembodied Mind."[11] Russell himself went to left wing extremes both in his politics and his behaviour in his response to the horrors of WW1. From a personal point of view, he saw little point in exercising virtue and became a notorious womanizer.

> The war of 1914-18 changed everything for me. I ceased to be academic and took to writing a new kind of books. I changed my whole conception of human nature. I became for the first time deeply convinced that Puritanism does not make for human happiness. . . . I saw that reformers and reactionaries alike in our present world have

become distorted by cruelties. I grew suspicious of all purposes demanding stern discipline.[12]

It is remarkable that Russell's autobiography up to the end of WW1 is teeming with convivial activity. He is constantly meeting and talking to people. After WW1, he is increasingly on his own and struggling to make sense of his life in an entirely different way. During the 1920s, he went to Russia and China presumably in search of answers but found none that satisfied him. Similarly, Lawrence went on his travels throughout the world, leaving a fruitful trail of novels in his wake.

Neither Russell nor Lawrence were being true to humanism when they rubbished opposing views because they were opposed to them. They saw each other's views as being intrinsically evil and thought that the world would be a better place without such views. In short, they wished to see them eradicated from the face of the Earth. Clearly they did not subscribe to Voltaire's famous saying: "I disapprove of what you say, but I will defend to the death your right to say it."[13] They reacted emotionally against each other's views to the point of wilfully misunderstanding them.

The humanist way is surely to try to understand why people need to adopt such radically opposing views to one's own. This is why the dualist view is important to the development of humanism. It provides a systematic way of understanding the import of diametrically opposing views. Thus, the humanist consensus is only possible when it can accommodate such opposing views by giving a sense of purpose to which most people can subscribe. They can sideline the extremists because it is obvious to them that the bigger picture involves both sides working together for better future instead of fighting against each other to no purpose whatsoever.

How the humanist consensus was lost

The falling out between Russell and Lawrence was symptomatic of the loss of the humanist consensus which had been threatening European civilization long before WW1. The latter event brought matters to a head because people were traumatized by the senseless loss of life it had caused. They lost faith decisively in the progress of humanity. But the seeds of that doubt were already taking root during the nineteenth century.

At its most potent, the humanist consensus had brought about the great intellectual movements of the Renaissance and the Enlightenment. These movements petered out as progress was usually slower than people's expectations. Their idealist belief in humanity's potential was worn away by the realities of life. The certainties of dogmatism reasserted themselves in the form of religion or ideology. Such certainties offered people the comfort and security they craved. During the nineteenth century, the split between left and right was widened by the rise of liberal and idealist philosophies that were mutually incompatible with each other.

Until the late nineteenth century, the humanist consensus had supported a secularist society of which religion was only a part and not the most dominant part. The extremes of capitalism were also tempered by improving working conditions and increasing wage levels for workers. The political aspirations of both the left and right therefore were moderated and pointed in humanist directions. However, during the nineteenth century, European thinking came under the thrall of two opposing philosophies: (1) a liberal, utilitarian philosophy emanating from Britain and (2) a conservative, idealist philosophy stemming from continental Europe.

The liberal philosophy had been championed by the Benthamites,[14] including John Stuart Mill (1806-1873), the most enduring beacon of liberalism.[15] But by the end of the nineteenth century, idealist philosophy held sway, even over Great Britain. Indeed, Bertrand Russell had begun his intellectual career at Cambridge University as an idealist philosopher, until G.E. Moore's influence led him back to his liberalist beginnings.[16]

German idealism of the early 20th century century was taken up in Great Britain later in the century. Philosophers such as T. H. Green (1836-1882), F. H. Bradley, (1846-1903), and John Mactaggart (1866-1925) espoused a British Hegelian philosophy that brought idealism to the fore. The fashionable sway of idealist thinking at this time amplified imperialist and jingoist sentiments. The European population was brainwashed into the adulation of 'God, King and Country' and this motivated millions of young men to march stubbornly into the mass massacres of WW1. These high ideals had become more real and important than human beings. Such Platonist thinking sullied the humanist consensus that the Enlightenment had nurtured so successfully. Thus, by 1914, the Platonist ideals of God, King and Country unified Europe sufficiently to justify a senseless war between self-congratulatory nations each of which had their own selfish and mutually incompatible imperialist ambitions.

Post-WW1, there was an immediate reaction against these imperialist ideals and, in the post-war chaos, many people went to the political extremes of the left and right. The communists and fascists came to power in Russia and Italy respectively, followed in the 1930s by the Nazis in Germany. These extremists were only interested in the exercise of power and in subjugating their respective peoples. The optimism of the humanist consensus had no place in their thinking. In contrast, the USA was still largely under the influence of the pragmatic philosophy of William James (1842-1910), John Dewey (1859-1952) and others. American optimism pervaded Europe to some extent post-WW1 and helped to moderate the pessimism and disillusion spawned by the senselessness of the war. American influence increased still further after World War Two and helped to reinstate the humanist consensus in Europe. This reached its crescendo during the nineteen sixties.

How to restore the humanist consensus

After WW2 and until the 1960s, the humanist consensus flourished once more in Europe and an air of general optimism swept the continent. Everything seemed possible, and even the Roman Catholic stooped to reforming and modernizing itself to some extent. But all that was brought to an end by the aimless political extremism of the late sixties both in Europe and the USA. Western civilisation lost its focus and no coherent humanist philosophy emerged to consolidate the consensus, and it faded away amidst the bromide of the seventies.

In short, the humanist consensus can only be restored by strengthening humanism so that it becomes the dominant view in society. I have already suggested in the section above on 'Dualism and Humanism' that this strengthening can be achieved by developing a dualist theory that ensures extremist thinking is avoided in our thinking. But extremist thinking is also avoided by looking at things from different perspectives. This is a contextual view that emphasizes putting things into wider contexts and not confining them to one context. An extremist may think that everything must be seen within the context of his or her religion or ideology. To them, no other context matters in life and they act accordingly.

Thus, avoiding the extremes of religious and idealist thinking requires us to develop a contextual theory which helps us broaden our perspective beyond ourselves and our egotistical concerns. What seems real, important and indubitable in one context can seem trivial and mean in another context. For example, buying new clothes for a job interview may seem vitally important in the context of one's daily life, but it is fairly unimportant in the context of world poverty in which many people worry about having something to eat, let alone what clothes to wear. The plight of the poor become of personal importance to us when we see things in that perspective – 'no man is an island entire of itself'.[17] This contextual view deals with how contexts take us out of our immediate concerns so that we see things in broader contexts, and remote events enter our sphere of thinking. This view is not new though it has never been properly explicated before in a philosophical manner. It is presaged, for example, in this quotation from the Italian philosopher, Giambattista Vico (1668-1744):

> In his bestial state, a man loves only his own well-being. After he takes a wife and has children, he continues to love his own well-being, and comes to love the well-being of his family as well. After he enters civil life, he comes to love the well-being of his city. After his city extends its rule over other peoples, he comes to love to the well-being of his nation. And

after such nations are united through war, peace, alliances, and trade, he comes to love the well-being of the entire human race. In all these contexts, the individual continues to love his own advantage above all else.[18]

Vico's view probably influenced that great Italian patriot, Giuseppe Mazzini (1805-1872), in his formulating the slogan, *Amate l'Umanità!* (love humanity!) which he used in his nineteenth century campaign to unify Italy's disparate nations and city states.[19] He considered the interests of humanity to be more important than those of family and country. The creation of a united Italy was more vital to humanity than loyalty to smaller units which were perpetually in conflict with each other. The context of humanity thus incorporates the other contexts such as family and nation to unify people when they open their minds to the importance of that viewpoint.

If humanity is to have a future we need to use such contexts to unify people of all political persuasions to get things done, such as reforming the global financial system and tackling climate change, which may be vital to the future of life let as well as humanity. I further argue that using dualist interaction helps us to make the best possible use of contexts. It means interacting with the contents of contexts on a one-to-one basis. Everything is not considered within the bounds of one point of view but is extended to include opposing views. We are thereby less more prone to go to dogmatic extremes since we are deliberately putting our problems in their proper perspectives and not making more of them than they really deserve. For example, humanists may find extreme religious views objectionable but that does not mean that they are so intolerant of them that they take violent action against people holding such views. They are more concerned with understanding why people can get into these mindsets than with eliminating them nazi-style. From a humanist point of view, the 'final solution' to the religious problem must to provide viewpoints that give people the moral, spiritual and philosophical support which at present they can only find in religion.

From a humanist point of view, there is no need for high, inhuman ideals to live up to, such as religion and ideology thump into us to the exclusion of everything else. But we do need parameters within which to function and gauge our behaviour. We can elevate ourselves and have confidence in our views because we are taking account of opposing views and are not claiming to have the whole truth and nothing but the truth. Thus, to unify people, the humanist answer must be interactive and contextual. This approach is exemplified by reference to a contextualization process that involves embracing different contextual outlooks. By this means, we train our minds to see different perspectives that are more all embracing. This is important for promoting the humanist consensus that depends so much on seeing things from different points of view. If we are to tolerate differences we must be able to appreciate the viewpoints that give rise to these differences. This contextualization process is now discussed in terms of a particular set of contexts. .

How to contextualize the problems of humanity

A process of **contextualization** is advocated here to unify us as individuals as regards matters that concern us as human beings. This process helps us to broaden our thinking to embrace different viewpoints. The contextualization process therefore involves putting ourselves into contexts wider than our narrow selfish contexts of everyday life. By seeing things from the same viewpoint as other people, we connect with them and we become at one with each other in that respect. We do this quite naturally when we feel guilty at the sight of starving children in the underdeveloped world or when we sympathize with people being killed for demonstrating against oppressive regimes. This contextual view enables us to make philosophical sense of these feelings and thus universalize them. They are made part of our rational thinking about ourselves and our role in this world. The more that we reason out our problems, the more we are able to cope with them and ultimately to solve them. Such reasonings make us more secure about the future, and the humanist consensus depends on the ubiquity of such optimistic thinking.

It is also important for humanists to promote the contextualization process because, for example, god-belief tends to de-contextualize people's thinking. God-belief is a form of de-contextualization in which all contextual thinking is reduced to a divine outlook. Any human outlook is subordinated to the divine one. In other words, unless people put their thoughts into wider contexts, such as those exemplified here, they will not see any further than God. All the wider contexts need to be seen in relation to each other and not to the exclusion of all the others, as in the case of God-belief. We are nothing compared to that entity therefore there is no logical reason for our doing anything for ourselves. It is all in the hands of God whatever we do. We need to be able to move to other contexts and see that the God context is not the only admissible one. This means believing that God is not the be-all and end-all of everything. We come into our own and start believing in ourselves. This is when the humanist view comes to the fore, and it is killed off whenever we think of God entering into everything to the point that we have no freewill and everything is pre-ordained by God. Thus, the humanist consensus cannot thrive for long in an environment where god-belief is the only admissible outlook.

Contextualization is important because we need to move between contexts and not be stuck in one context at the expense of all the others. If we are not flexible in our thinking in this context manner, we become narrow-minded, obsessive, fanatical, extremist, unbalanced or distorted in our thinking in some way. Most of the problems of the world result from people being stuck in one context or another so that they are unable to appreciate the importance of other points of view. Religious extremism and ideological bigotry are examples of such distort thinking.

Contextualization helps us to make connections between contexts and move between them. We connect with other people and society in general by seeing things from the same viewpoint. We can also move from one viewpoint to another by entering different contexts. This process brings us all together and unifies us as a species so that we can move forward instead of falling out with each other as we are too prone to do. This is why contextualization is essential to the humanist consensus being advocated here.

For the purposes of this paper, this contextualization process is illustrated by reference to the following connecting contexts: **reality, ideality, famility, sociality, humanity, vitality** and **futurity**.[20] These connecting, unifying contexts help us to find meaning in our lives and to unify us as human beings within wider spheres of activity. They ensure we do not live for self alone. They connect us with other people who also can enter into the same points of view. When we think of the plight of other people we do so from their perspective and therefore enlarge our own thinking beyond our selfish concerns. Thus, the selfish person can learn to be less selfish when they realise that their own perspective is not necessarily the most important one.

All these contexts are included within the context of humanity since we can only think about things as human beings. We cannot realistically think outside the human box into which we are born and habitually function. We might imagine how alien beings might think or feel but that is only with the context of ideality. No matter how imaginative our ideas are, they remain merely human ideas since all our ideas are founded on our human experience. Until we actually meet alien intelligent beings we can only think of them from our perspective which is irremediably human.

In common with all contexts, these connecting contexts are distinct from our notions of them. When we conceive of them as notions, we are thinking of their language usage. We define notions by showing how distinct they are from each other. But contexts are functions of our thinking about things in general rather than about particular objects of language. For example, in the context of love we need not think about our own experiences of loving relationships whereas our notion of love must be founded to some extent on our own loving relationships. Contexts embrace our thoughts expressed in words but are not expressed themselves in words when they are in use. When we contextualize our thinking, the contexts provide the areas within which we think about things. They transcend language usage and constitute the framework for our thinking in notions and conceptions. Our words and symbols lack lasting meaning and reference unless they are expressed within some context or other.

Contexts also differ from our notions of them in that they are intimately interrelated. They are inseparable in that each context is contained within the others, and the others are all contained within it. The contents of contexts are shared with each of them and therefore they cannot be usefully separated or logically analyzed as if they were distinct from each other. We interact with and within contexts in such a way that each of them can contain all the rest. Thus, for example, the contexts of futurity and reality can respectively contain all the rest as depicted in the following diagrams:

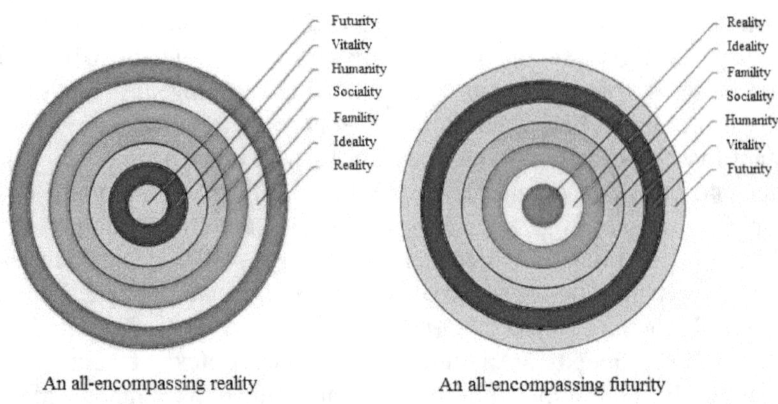

An all-encompassing reality   An all-encompassing futurity

Reality is the default context within which we all live from one second to the second. It contains all other contexts but only animals may live entirely within that context to the exclusion of all others. When we think about what we are experiencing then we inevitably enter into a context within reality. A parent looking at his or her child will have thoughts and feelings about looking after their child that are not perceivable in reality. They are subjective experiences and therefore in the contexts of ideality and familiy. Nevertheless, they are in the context of reality as they refer to real objects, namely, their children. Thus, reality is all one thing in our direct experience of but we can only think of bits of it at any moment in time. We narrow the context when we think about anything at all. But as long as we stay in touch with reality we remain within that context. Animals, on the other hand, may have real experiences that are nothing but real in so far as they have no thoughts of anything beyond that which they are directly perceiving.

When we look to the future, we enter the context of futurity within which all the other contexts are contained, but only while we are in that frame of mind. Thus, when a family thinks ahead to next year's holidays, it puts itself into the context of futurity and imagines the reality of what might occur during that holiday – the quality of the hotel, the reliability of flights, the political situation of the country to be visited, and so on. The problems of society can only be solved in the future and therefore must be considered in the context of futurity. On the other hand, our thoughts of the future are subject to ideal imagini unless they are contained within the context of reality. Within that context we take the most realistic view of matters by making use of our hard-earned past experiences when things have turned out contrary to our expectations. Similarly, the other contexts can be depicted as containing all the others depending on the circumstances in which they are used.

When we are thinking about the family alone then all other contexts are seen from the famility point of view in so far as we are thinking deeply enough about it. Similarly, in thinking about life in general, we see it from the point of view of vitality as herein defined. We therefore move from one contextual totality to another when we think about different things. If we do not include all other points of view within the context in mind, we are narrow-minded and superficial in our thinking to that extent. Thus, contextualization helps us to broaden our minds and take account of all other points of view, potentially in a holistic fashion.

The contextualization process therefore describes what we do quite naturally without thinking of what we do in these terms. These connecting contexts are among the most crucial contexts within which we habitually function without being overly conscious of the fact. Within them we arrive at meaningful conceptions by which to make sense of our lives and give them meaning and purpose. Thinking about these contexts in an abstract way ensures that they become more impersonal and manipulable. They are tools that usefully give us more control over ourselves and help us to interrelate more effectively with the external world. Putting ourselves into these contexts takes us out of ourselves and places us in the widest possible contexts. Otherwise we tend to make too much or too little of them. For example, a family man may become too involved with his family or too little. With more thought of about his position *vis-à-vis* more encompassing contexts, he realizes that the future of his family depends not just on his actions and resources but also on what happens in society.

These contexts are crucial to us because they go to the crux of the matter as regards what we can or cannot do with ourselves. They are all-encompassing, long-standing, and fundamental in comparison with most other contexts. They are more fundamental than the more personal contexts of the self in that we live our lives within them even if we do nothing else with our lives. Everyone learns to face reality, has ideas of their own, has family relations, participates in the sociality of other people, has vitality of their own, thinks about humanity and looks to the future. It is what they do whenever they do meaningful and worthwhile things with their lives that are judged to be so within these contexts.

These contexts are more abstract than the most of the other contexts and they are learnt as part of the socializing process rather than being absorbed through the normal use of language. They evince themselves on our becoming mature and responsible adults who are able to relate themselves to the whole human race, the whole of life and ultimately the whole universe. In this way, contextualization helps us to be more holistic and all-encompassing in our thinking about everything.

These contexts are also useful in clarifying problems such as the relationship of science to religion. Scientific theories are obviously more meaningful within the context of science than in the context of religion. But they are also more meaningful within the context of external reality than religious beliefs. The latter are best understood within the contexts of ideality and sociality.

Clarifying the connecting contexts

The role of these contexts can be clarified by outlining what they mean. This clarification is suggestive of how they function independently of each other, even though in practice they are rarely so distinct in their usage. They are outlined as follows:

Reality

Within this context everything 'out there' is contextualized to make sense of things as being real or not being real. In other words, everything is put into that context when we realize the reality of what we apprehend as existing 'out there'. The context of reality contains other contexts such as perceived reality and physical reality which contribute to the contents of external reality. Thus, tables and chairs exist in the context of perceived reality but not in the context of physical reality as laid down by physicists. In the latter context, material objects are largely empty space with a scattering of interacting force fields. The content of external reality in everyday life also includes our schools, hospitals, cars, superstars, participation in games and every other externalized aspect of our culture, in so far as they exist as physical objects or as physical activity. Thus, everything that happens out there and makes sense to us, comprises external reality because we are able to put them in that context. We have to contextualize its contents depending on the view we take of them or the use we make of them.

Moreover, the contents of external reality are quantifiable and measurable in physical terms. Thus, Locke's 'primary qualities' of 'bulk, figure, extension, number, and motion of solid parts'[21] are really measurable quantities. Even his secondary qualities of 'colour, sound, taste, etc.,' have become measurable through the progress of physics, though they were not so in his day. In so far as the latter are measurable, they differ from our vivid subjective experiences of them. What we experience as colours and tastes do not really exist in the way we experience them. They are as much ideal as real in the way we experience them. Thus, what is contained in the context of external reality is distinct from what is experienced in the context of ideality. The former are quantifiable as compared with the qualitative nature of ideality.

We often think of aspects of our culture as being 'real'. Games, races and other sporting activities seem real enough. Art and music are real parts of our culture. But all such cultural activities also belong to other contexts such as ideality and sociality in an interactive way. Their physical reality is strictly limited to equipment, instruments, buildings, clothing and other artefacts. If we confine them entirely to the context of reality then we are liable to make too much of them. We become enslaved to them as true fanatics and disciples. Thus, extremism of this kind is avoided when we put things in their proper context depending on the circumstances of our experience of them.

More than perception is required to establish what is real or not real. We need clear ideas and concepts by which to make sense of what is perceived. In our immediate experience, we immediately conceive external reality to be what it is **on the whole**, and not in terms of its complex contents. We fill in the details concerning what really exists by other means than perception, for example, by thinking, judging, remembering, or by social means, such as consulting others or conducting scientific research. We arrive at the truth as to what really exists by similar extrinsic activity and this invariably means verifying or falsifying what is thought to exist or not thought to exist.

The full story of what really exists is unending one. Despite their quantifiability, measurability and their common sense basis, the contents of external reality are potentially as problematic as the contents of other contexts (1) because of the fallibility of our senses and thinking powers and (2) because we cannot always agree amongst ourselves concerning the precise content of external reality even when we are all witnessing the same scene. There can be no end to what can said about what really exists or what really does not exist. Thus, to do justice to the context of external reality would require more than a book or two.

Ideality

As we are mere human beings we cannot abide being bogged down in reality all the time. We need to free our thoughts from the bitter hear-and-now and use our imagination and pursue our dreams however far-fetched. Then we resort to the context of ideality in which we are dealing with the ideal and not just the real.

Compared with reality, the context of ideality exists potentially but not actually. The ideas passing through our minds give rise to an ideality which is the collective name used here for our ideal thinking as a whole. Ideality is not the same as subjectivity which is contrasted with objectivity. What is subjective is ideal but not everything that is ideal is subjective because ideas can be independent of our subjective experiencing of them. They subsist as potentially interactive entities even though they do not exist in reality. This applies when ideas are used in a social context in which they are actively used by other people.

Thus, our own ideas are not actually distinct from the thoughts passing through our heads at any given moment. But their potential existence enables us to treat ideality as an objective repository that provides us with ideas, notions, conceptions, intuitions, insights, contexts, perspectives, contexts, and so on. That objective repository (called 'World 3' by Karl Popper[22]) is what we have in common with others. In so far as ideality is personal to each of us, it requires constant tempering in relation to external reality on the one hand and social scrutiny on the other hand. Thus, ideality is an interactive process that can never be pinned down in the mind.

The contents of ideality are generally qualitative in so far as they involve evaluative judgments of one kind or another. Things can be valued by using evaluative notions such as good, beauty, and justice. Ideality is inclusive just as external reality is exclusive. It operates by including our thoughts and ideas by means of the 'axiom of internal relations', to use Hegelian terminology. Thus, by moving into a context or perspective we include everything pertinent to it, and its content is ideal unless we do things as agents that will confirm the real existence of the content in external reality, for instance, by perceiving, experimenting, researching, or asking other people.

Famility

Famility refers to the whole idea of the togetherness of families in which people relate closely to each other whether or not there is any biological linkage. As a notion, it includes not just the nuclear or extended family but also all our friendships and the other familiar relationships that fill our lives. Everyone with whom we are familiar may be regarded with famility. We are all born into the famility framework in the shape of a family life that helps each of us to establish our individuality. The first social realities that we must face in life consist in understanding how we are same as or different from other family members. We establish our own identity in that way.

Having family roots is necessary to our security and peace of mind. We establish our emotional base in our family upbringing. Thus, breaking free of family roots is difficult for us all. In forming friendships outside the family, we expand the famility framework and prepare ourselves to enter the context of sociality that includes society as a whole. We extend our famility sphere when we successively go to school, university, become employees, create our own family and so on. In a tribal society, the tribe as a whole functions as famility. In a complex, modern society, we need the notion of famility to take over from the old tribal or clan affinities. Famility therefore fazes smoothly or otherwise into the sphere of sociality.

Sociality

Within the context of sociality, all our social activities take place, including family activities. Thus, human relationships in general take place within this context. All our knowledge is focused on it as the repository of knowledge and understanding. It is also a sphere of activity within which our knowledge and understanding is communicated and perpetuated. We increase our knowledge within the context of sociality, for example, by talking to people, using the internet, conducting businesses, taking educational courses, and so on. Society is the abstract idea of human beings participating in a unified culture, while the sociality is the context within which society as a whole functions. Our families, groups and organisations participate in the sociality, and in so far as they set themselves apart from it, they are potentially inimical to its unity and purpose. For example, the notion of the internet becomes more meaningful when we think of it as operating within the context of the sociality which embraces all human communication. It is no longer seen solely as something private to ourselves, friends and family as it involves all humanity.

Humanity

Humanity contains all other contexts in so far as we cannot avoid being human beings doing human things. The context of humanity is particularly important in uniting us as a species against the racial, national, religious, sectarian and economic divisions that forever threaten to turn us against each other in self-destructive war and conflict. We have no future unless humanity as a whole pulls together with its collective future in mind. When we all put ourselves in the context of humanity, we can be united by the common aims of humanity. This happens when we empathize with our fellow human beings who are afflicted by famines, pandemics, earthquakes, tsunamis, terrorist attacks and so on. It is an additional dimension of ourselves, and an expression of our human feelings. It is not the same as the idea of humanity which has been misused by utopian ideologists to justify killing and torturing their fellow human beings. In that case, the idea has become more important than people and is treated in an absolutist way. By treating humanity as context like any other, we do not put it above and beyond us but make an intimate part of what we are as individuals. It is concerned with our sympathetic feelings about other people and not with our thinking of them in an abstract and inhuman way. Their lives are more important than any abstract ideas because their vitality is even more important than their humanity.

Vitality

Vitality is the context in which we live our lives to the full in common with all other living beings. In that context we appreciate the importance of life and living. We thereby develop the inner strength of will to keep going against the odds because we regard our lives and the lives of all life-forms as being significant in themselves. It is more important than humanity in that life in some form will continue on this planet even though humanity disappears from it entirely. Thus, embracing this context helps us to empathize with other life-forms and it encourages us to preserve life for its own sake. In this context, the purpose of humanity is to protect, promote and propagate life, and to make more of it than previously existed. However this purpose is not to be pursued dogmatically or in total isolation from our personal needs and those of other people.

Those who fail to enter into the context of vitality as part of their thinking will not appreciate the value of life. They will lack the inner strength to withstand the vicissitudes of life since they lack sufficient reasons to live and make something of their lives.[23] They will find it difficult if not impossible to adopt and maintain a 'live and let live' policy as life itself has less meaning to them. They will dispute the fact that other life-forms and indeed other people have a right to live their lives in their own way. They know themselves to be living but they have no means of valuing their own lives, let alone those of others. The only view they can appreciate is a reductive view which focuses on the content and existence of life and not on the value of life as a whole. Their narrow view of life is such that they are liable to take life in the name of life instead of valuing all life. Thus, it is necessary for us enter with our thoughts into this context to relate ourselves fully to life as a whole.

Futurity

Futurity is the context of future consequences. Future generations are important to us because everything we do now has some consequence to futurity. All our rational and purposeful activities gravitate towards the context of futurity within which the value of those activities is ultimately assessed. Futurity ultimately involves all other contexts because everything which occurs within them has some consequence or other within the context of futurity. Everything that we do now, at this very moment, has some further meaning in the future which cannot be ascertained in the present. If we want to understand, for example, where the sociality is going in the far future, we can only do so from the perspective of futurity. The following diagram illustrates to the tendency of these connecting contexts towards futurity.

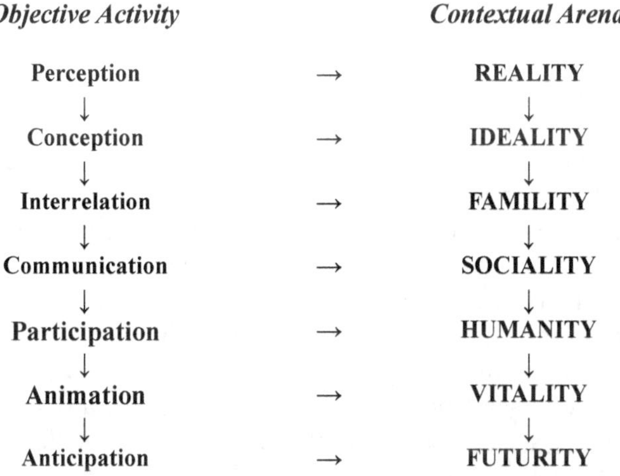

The Directional Flow of the Connecting Contexts

The connecting contexts are therefore directional in that they all point towards the far future. What we perceive now is used to govern our actions in the future. I see a taxi approaching and hail it with the intention of boarding it. Our perceptions can also be communicated to others to influence their future actions. I see a car approaching and I warn a friend not to step off the sidewalk. At any point in the present we can do no more than anticipate, predict, and foretell the future. But in entering into the context of futurity we inevitably arrive at insights and conclusions which influence our behaviour for better or for worse in the present. Not all our future thoughts occur within the context of ideality. Our plans often pan out quite realistically because we have carefully accounted for all the eventualities in making these plans.

Thus, even in moving towards the future, contexts are connected in a closed loop. On learning that a concert is taking place on a certain date in the fuure, you may change your plans in the present to obtain for yourself and friends tickets to that concert. You have unknowingly entered into all of these contexts in completing that task. The reality of a concert taking place gives rise to the idea of attending it. Thinking of friends involves famility, obtaining tickets occurs within sociality. Concert-going takes place in the context of humanity, and is a way of our expressing our vitality. We are therefore thinking through all these contexts in our everyday activities such as concert-going. Thus, we add to our self-knowledge by understanding better the role of these contexts in our everyday thinking about things.

How contextualization involves dualist interaction

The connecting contexts can only be properly understood as an application of dualist theory. This is in addition their use in formal logic or any other form of analysis, dualist theory provides an additional outlook that complements the latter. In other words, their functioning involves dualist interaction and they cannot subsist independently of such interactions. They are not being analysed or treated like discrete, objective entities. Reality as a connecting context depends on a constant interaction between our subjective experiences of reality and our objective positing of reality as something entirely independent of us. The dualist interactions involved in these particular contexts are outlined in the diagram on the next page.

We are in the context of reality when we interact with the contents of reality by means of perception, trial-and-error, experimentation, when seeking the facts, searching for evidence or what is really the case. By such interactions we seek to eliminate the subjective in our thinking and reach as much objectivity of which we are humanly capable. The scientific method usually consists in an interaction between the subjective and objective which is basically what the so-called 'hypothetico-deductive' method involves. What is posited hypothetically is largely subjective until its consequences are deduced and tested in relation to reality. This is obviously an interactive process of trial-and-error which may never reach a definite or long-lasting conclusion.

In using our imagination, thinking and planning ahead, or dreaming about possibilities, we are invariably functioning within the context of ideality wherein we can be sure that whatever we are thinking has no immediate basis in reality. Our thoughts are also personal to ourselves when we are not communicating them to other people, recording them or writing them down. Whenever we attempt to establish a real basis for these thoughts then the context of reality comes into play, and ideality is suborned within that context.

The context of famility is necessarily entwined with that of reality as we have constantly to face the reality of one's relationships with other people to maintain our familiarity with them as people. These relationships are deeply personal to us because we depend on the affection and reciprocity that friends and family give us. The extent to which our relationships turn out to be subjective and are not reciprocated means that a constant process of social interaction is required to maintain and repair our relationships.

The context of sociality is therefore intricately interwoven with that of famility since the functioning of society and its organisations depends on friendship and co-operation between people who might not always agree with or even like each other very much. Thus, within the context of sociality, professional relationships are very important since they do not require the same degree of familiarity as more intimate relationships. They depend more on good manners and respect for the individual *qua* individual than on familiarity for its own sake.

Types of Interaction	Methods	Contexts
Objective/Subjective	Perception Trial and Error Scientific Method	**Reality**
Subjective/Personal	Personal Insight Creativity Improvization	**Ideality**
Personal/Familiar	Affection Family Security	**Famility**
Familiar/Social	Friendship Co-operation Organization	**Social**
Social/Human	Tolerance Compassion Empathy	**Humanity**
Human/Resilience	Liveliness Development Evolution	**Vitality**
Resilience/Advancement	Anticipation Planning Foresight	**Futurity**

The Contexts of Particular Dualist Interactions

However, these contexts are to no avail if society has no future. Within the context of futurity, we ensure that we have a future by planning ahead and thinking about future consequences of all our actions. This is a prospectivist way of thinking in which we try to use our past experiences to make our future better. This compares with a retrospective way of thinking that habitually reconstructs the past in the present and avoids changing things in the future (see the next section of this book for more on these distinctions). Only within the context of futurity can we have the foresight we need for our survival as a species.

These connecting contexts will subsist and be useful for as long as human beings or intelligent beings exist to make use of them. They will be here for as long as we or our successors are here. Though the existence of these contexts is inherently stable, their content is in constant flux. In being continually active in respect of such contexts we keep our minds open to constant updating. Their importance lies especially in their countering relativism. They provide long-lasting standpoints by which lasting judgments can be made. But these standpoints are not absolute and inviolable; their content can be changed in response to new circumstances. For example, the protection of primitive cultures must be considered within the context of humanity as a whole. Their right as a culture to be different must be balanced with their right as individuals to have all the trappings and opportunities available in a developed modern culture. This means that their culture cannot be hived off from the rest of humanity. For the people's sake, their culture must evolve in an orderly fashion to incorporate all the benefits of modern culture. Humanity is the standpoint but within that context there is scope for differences and for changes in the future.

Conclusion

The humanist consensus is a fragile thing that waxes and wanes with the spirit of the times. Fashionable thinking often militates against it. Political or religious extremism of any kind can destroy it or downgrade it in the public eye. We seem to be entering a period in which optimism about our future is dwindling. Extremist thinking is swirling into the vacuum left by our failure to renew and strengthen the humanist consensus. I have suggested here and elsewhere that the development of dualist theory is one way of reinstating the humanist consensus and of renewing our faith in humanity's abilities to tackle and overcome whatever problems it faces. By learning to put ourselves into the appropriate contexts, we bring ourselves into the bigger picture. We see things as a whole and can take the long term view. Unless we plan for a better future there will be no future for us. Putting ourselves in the appropriate contexts such as the connecting contexts outlined in this paper helps us to broaden our minds. It will hopefully allow new insights and ways of thinking to come to our aid.

Seeing things anew can instil hope within us. Unless we have hope in our hearts for a better future, there will be none.

Notes and References

1. Bertrand Russell (1872-1970) established analytical philosophy as the dominant philosophy of the 20th century, and D.H. Lawrence (1885-1930) wrote innumerable novels which are still widely read and some have been made into notable feature films such as *Women in Love*.

2. D. H. Lawrence, *Kangaroo*. (1925), London: Penguin Books, 1980, ch.12, p. 240.

3. The Bloomsbury set was associated with the house of Virginia Woolf's father, Leslie Stephen (1832-1904) in Bloomsbury Square, London, not far from the British Museum.

4. Ronald W. Clark, *The Life of Bertrand Russell*. Harmondsworth: Penguin, 1975, ch. 10, pp. 323-326.

5. Bertrand Russell, *The Autobiography of Bertrand Russell*. (1967), London: Allen & Unwin, 1975, Volume Two, ch. 8, p. 243.

6. Ibid. p.244.

7. Harry T. Moore, *The Priest of Love: A Life of D.H. Lawrence*. Revised edition, 1974. Harmondsworth: Penguin Books, 1976, part three, ch. 6, p. 372.

8. Ibid., part four, ch. 8, p. 491.

9. Terry Eagleton, *The English novel: An Introduction*. Wiley-Blackwell, 2005, pp. 258–260.

10. D. H. Lawrence, *Apocalypse*. (1931), Penguin, 1974, p. 125.

11. Harry T. Moore, ibid., part five, ch. 1, p. 516.

12. Russell, ibid., p. 261

13. This saying is attributed to Voltaire by S.G. Tallentyre in *Friends of Voltaire* (1907), p. 199.

14. Followers of Jeremy Bentham (1748-1832), the founder of the Utilitarian movement which itself was based on the ethical views of David Hume. James Mill (1773-1836), the father of John Stuart Mill, was perhaps Bentham's most devoted follower.

15. J. S. Mill's famous essay, *On Liberty* (1859), is the classic statement of what liberalism is about.

16. Ibid., ch. 5. p. 136. George Edward Moore (1873-1958) together with Russell founded the analytical movement that dominated philosophy in the 20th century.

17. John Donne (1572-1631), 'Devotions upon Emergent Occasions – Meditation XVII' (1624). *Selected Prose*, Penguin Books, 1987, p. 126.

18. Giambatista Vico, *New Science*. (1744), London: Penguin, 1999, Section Four, §341, pp. 125-126.

19. Giuseppe Mazzini, *The Duties of Man*, London: J.M. Dent & Co., 1955, pp. 49-50.

20. The nature of such contexts and their application are further clarified in my forthcoming book, *Our Dualist Mentality: An Outline of the Dualist Way of Thinking.*

21. John Locke, *An Essay Concerning Human Understanding*, (1690-1710), Oxford: Clarendon Press, 1979, ed. P.H. Nidditch, Book II, ch. IX, §26, pp. 142-143.

22. Karl Popper, *Objective Knowledge*, Oxford: Oxford University Press, 1975, ch. 3, pp. 106-107, and ch. 4, pp. 153-154.

23. There is more about strengthening the will and find reasons for living in my book, *The Will to Live: A Systematic Guide to our Reasons for Living* (Almostic Publications, 2014).

Part Three

Economics

IX. Henry Ford: The Visionary Humanist

Abstract

This paper contains (1) an outlined portrait of Henry Ford, warts and all, (2) a summary of his 'humane capitalism', the importance of which has been largely forgotten nowadays, and (3) a suggestion of its relevance to today's economic problems. Ford's importance as a humanist becomes obvious when his view of capitalism is compared with that of his predecessor, Andrew Carnegie. Ford reacted implicitly against Carnegie's draconian capitalism in which poverty was seen as an unavoidable necessity. In Carnegie's view, wages could be lowered at an employer's whim. Ford overturned that view and made increasing wage levels the norm not the exception. He was in fact directly responsible for the development of the consumer society during the twentieth century.

"It is a shock when the mind awakens to the fact that not all of humanity is human – that whole groups of people do not regard others with humane feelings."

– **Henry Ford (1922)**[1]

1. Introduction

Henry Ford, this essay argues, was a humanist who changed the world for the better. He was not particularly brilliant, knowledgeable or articulate, but he knew his own mind and what he wanted done.

He had a humanist vision of a society in which the standard of living of everyone would be gradually improved and poverty would be gradually reduced. That vision was put into practice to a large extent during the twentieth century, and it resulted in the consumer society in which most people had more money to spend and sufficient leisure time to pursue their own interests. The humane capitalism which Ford popularized led to more efficient and precise ways of lowering costs in large-scale organizations. It also ensured that there was a trickle down effect that benefited workers and improved industrial relations.

Ford did not think of himself as a humanist, as humanism in its present sense only developed from about 1920 onwards. He did, however, subscribe implicitly to the humanist consensus as mentioned in the previous section of this book. He believed in the value of the individual human being. He also believed that industry should serve humanity more than it should indulge in ruthless competition.

Ford's humanism contrasts with the inhumane form of capitalism that preceded him: what I call 'Carnegian capitalism', in which wage rates were actually lowered in cost cutting exercises thus causing unnecessary social strife. Ford's humane capitalism catered for human needs and aspirations whereas the latter was based primarily on Spencerian 'survival of the fittest' principles (Carnegie was a personal friend of the evolutionist philosopher Herbert Spencer). The former concerned what best supplied the needs of people whereas the latter was based on the dogmatic application of ideas and principles. Thus, Fordian capitalism was humane in comparison with Carnegian capitalism because it was human centred more than it was idea centred.

In spite of the success of Ford's vision, the profit motive remains the most prominent feature of contemporary capitalism. It is causing capitalism to go off the rails and lose its humanity in many respects. It is argued in this paper that Ford's view of capitalism needs to be reinforced and systematized, especially in respect of its humanist elements, if capitalism is to continue to be a successful economic basis for our society.

2. The importance of Ford's humanism

One of the most momentous events in human history occurred in 1914. This was not just the beginning of the war in Europe in August 1914, it was Henry Ford's announcement on 5th January 1914 that his company would almost double the wages of its car workers in Detroit and introduce an eight hour day. This event astonished the world and its success forced other industrialists to follow suit. It marked the beginning of the twentieth century's consumer society as it gave workers enough money in their pockets to freely consume products and to enjoy greater leisure time. It introduced the trickle-down effect of capitalism that ensured an improving standard of living for all workers and not just a privileged élite.

There was a humanist vision behind Ford's thinking and this eclipsed the inhumane capitalism that preceded it. It became the dominant view of capitalism for the rest of the twentieth century. The success of Ford's ideas in superseding what came before it, shows the importance of getting our ideas right if we are to change society for the better. Capitalism in general means using capital to make the highest profit by the most straightforward and legal methods possible. This leaves room for the antithesis of Ford's humane capitalism which I have called 'Carnegian capitalism' in honour of that great philanthropist and notorious strike-breaker, Andrew Carnegie.[2]

Carnegie tells us in his *Autobiography* that he was a friend and disciple of the philosopher, Herbert Spencer, whose social Darwinism he adopted as his religion in place of his native Calvinism. After reading some of Spencer's and Darwin's works, he comments: "Not only had I got rid of theology and the supernatural, but I had found the truth of evolution."[3] He therefore believed in 'survival of the fittest' and that people should struggle and fight to better themselves. In one of his published articles called "The Advantages of Poverty" (1891) he argues that it is more advantageous to struggle out of poverty, as he himself did, than to start from a position of comfort and security:

> Poor boys reared thus directly by their parents possess such advantages over those watched and taught by hired strangers, and exposed to the temptations of wealth and position, that it is not surprising they become the leaders in every branch of human action.[4]

In Carnegie's view, the workings of society depend on an absolute division between rich and poor so that poverty will always be with us. Without it, no one would have any incentive to enrich themselves. This view was later comprehensively overturned by Ford in his actions and in his writings.

In another article "An Employer's View of Labor" (1886), Carnegie laid down the steps required "in the advance towards permanent peaceful relations between capital and labor." The first of these steps states "That compensation be paid the men based upon a sliding scale in proportion to the prices received for product."[5] If the prices of the company's products go down, the wages of the workers producing the goods should decrease proportionately. He also argued that peaceful arbitration would eliminate the need for any strikes or lockouts, and that workers should be organised so that 'the leaders, the best men' came to the fore to negotiate with employers. This preference for 'the best men' meant that his most skilled technicians were highly paid and reputedly came to work in private carriages and wore top hats on pay day, while his semi-skilled workers lived on low wages and in most abject conditions of filth and squalor.[6] This is the inevitable consequence of the greedy 'dog eat dog' capitalism that even today is liable to rear its ugly head, as it did in the nineteen eighties and was depicted in the 'Wall Street' feature film in which the creed is greed and not the public good.

Carnegie's response to new technology in his steel mills, which cut costs and lowered prices, contrasts starkly with Ford's later policies. His sliding scale rule meant that wages were rigidly tied to prices, so that falling prices could not possibly accompany rising wages. The notorious Homestead strike of 1892 in Pittsburgh arose because workers' wages were to be cut according to Carnegie's sliding scale. While he sulked and skulked in Skibo Castle in Scotland, his manager, Henry Frick, applied his principles to the letter. On previous occasions, Carnegie himself had dismissed and locked out striking workers and replaced them with new men.[7] Frick was doing the same and he began by fortifying the mills with a twelve foot perimeter fence with holes for water hoses to be deployed. (The strikers called it 'Fort Frick'.)

Frick assembled over three hundred armed Pinkerton men whom he called 'watchmen' and whose function was to protect the property.[8] But the strikers prevented entry into the mills, and when the Pinkerton men arrived by barge, they were confronted with a mob of ten thousand people on the shore including women and children. In the ensuing clashes, some sixty men on both sides were shot and about thirty-five of them killed.[9] Frick was effectively dealing with the situation 'Wild West' style with a *posse comitatus* but, in the event, the sheriff's representative refused to deputize the Pinkerton men even when they came under fire.[10] They surrendered and were mistreated by the mob before being put on a train to Pittsburgh. Eventually the dispute ended peacefully when the Governor ordered 8,000 state militia to take over the mills. A Congressional Committee Report concluded that lives could have been saved if Frick had appealed to the Governor in the first place.[11]

Carnegie was out of touch with the real situation and would not accept blame for it. He wrote in his *Autobiography* that "the sheriff with guards" were needed to protect the three thousand workers, who were non-union, from the two hundred and eighteen workers who belonged to the union. The latter were led by "violent and aggressive men" who used guns and pistols "to intimidate the thousands."[12] The fact is that the Pinkerton men brought firearms in crates although their use without authority was strictly illegal.[13] Officially, Carnegie was distraught about the strike and its outlook. He wrote to Prime Minister W. E. Gladstone in these terms but privately he accused his underlings of bad tactics. They were doing the right thing but not subtly enough.[14] Basically, Carnegie thought that employers had the right to reduce or increase wages according to market vagaries. Unions got in the way of his social Darwinism therefore they had to be tamed if not eliminated. His company used its 'success' in the Homestead strike to reduce union power for decades afterwards.

Some two decades following these repressive measures, Henry Ford overturned Carnegian principles by pursuing diametrically opposite policies, such as increasing wages while reducing the prices of his products. Their implementation led to steady improvement in the living standard of ordinary people during the twentieth century. Nowadays, it is too easily forgotten the extent of our indebtedness to the humane capitalism proselytized by Ford. The consumer society, as we now know it, existed only in Ford's idealistic imagination in the first decade of the twentieth century. By the middle of the century, his consumerism had transformed Western society and, by the end of the century, it spanned the globe. It is therefore worthwhile looking at Ford the man and at the humanism that underlies his basic ideas.

Ford ought to be considered one of the greatest humanists in history. He clearly showed how humanist ideas can change the world for the better. But he has been largely ignored in recent years. Perhaps this is because he has been misunderstood and people have had extreme opinions of him. To the extreme left he seems to be an anti-Semitic autocratic plutocrat, and to the extreme right an anarchist / socialist / communist. Undoubtedly he was a human being with foils, foibles and failings like the rest of us. However, his achievements by far outweigh his faults, as I will now argue.

3. What was Ford really like?

Henry Ford began his working life with an elementary education and the mentality of a farm hand/garage mechanic. Through the university of life, he became a great guru who changed the world for the better. He compensated for his lack of education by using the expertise of men whom he enthused with his vision and drive. His close business associate Charles E. Sorenson tells us the following:

> Although he neglected his education as a boy, the business he developed taught him much. "What I don't know," he used to tell me, "I can always hire someone to show me how to do. In that way I learn more than if I tried to do it myself."[15]
>
> He would have gone nowhere without his associates, we did the work while he took the bows, yet none of us would have gone far without him. He has been described as complex, contradictory, a dreamer, a grown-up boy, an intuitive genius, a dictator, yet essentially he was a very simple man.[16]
>
> Henry Ford was no mystic or genius. He was a responsible person with determination to do his work as he believed it should be done. This sense of responsibility was one of his strongest traits.[17]
>
> This ability to sense signs of the times and to counteract forces that showed danger signals was almost uncanny. I would go to him with problems that looked insurmountable. Nothing appeared to frighten him.[18]
>
> By nature he was a happy person. Despite his lack of close friends and the aloof life he lived, he enjoyed being with a group of his men developing some project.[19]

Ford was not an easy man to work with. Sorenson relates that he delighted in playing cruel practical jokes on his top-level staff. For example, he would arrange for a telegram to be sent to them informing them of some disaster occurring at their plant, thus putting them into a state of fear and alarm until they realized they had been hoaxed.[20] But Sorenson thought that his good qualities far out-weighed his bad ones:

> Henry Ford was opinionated in matters about which he knew little or nothing. He could be small-minded, suspicious, jealous, and occasionally malicious and lacking in sincerity... These were his defects. Taken by themselves, they are grave faults, and it might be wondered how one could retain one's self-regard and still serve such a man. But when weighed against his good qualities, his sense of responsibility, his exemplary

personal life, and his far-reaching accomplishment, these defects become microscopic. It is not for his failings but for his impact upon his time and his momentous part in liberating men from backbreaking toil that he will stand out in the future. It was because I understood what he was trying to do that I pinned my flag on Henry Ford and that I still hold him in respect and esteem and am proud to have had the label "Henry Ford's man."[21]

Ford was a visionary but a relatively uneducated and unsophisticated one. He called himself "an ignorant idealist" during a court case in which he naively revealed his abysmal lack of education.[22] It appears that Ford was what we would now call 'dyslexic'. He was always uncomfortable reading anything.

> I was astonished how poor Henry Ford was at spelling. I never saw him write or dictate a letter. His secretaries, Ernest G. Liebold and Frank Campsall, prepared replies to communications which he had not even read. I have seen Liebold hold letters that had to be answered on his desk for days before he could catch Mr. Ford and read them to him. Ford didn't sign a letter very often – even left that to his secretaries.[23]

Ford was shy of speaking before more than a few people, and his abhorrence of public speaking hampered his attempt to become a senator, let alone president.[24] "He was a very good speaker with two or three people, just sitting round a table," recalled Fred L. Black, one of his close associates.[25]

In some ways, Ford was a philosopher *manqué*. But he reached philosophy mostly through the works of R. W. Emerson[26] and with his friendship with R. W. Trine. The more unconventional, if not bizarre, aspects of Ford's thinking featured in his published interviews with Trine and G. S. Viereck. Ralph Waldo Trine had achieved fame with the book, *In Tune with the Infinite*.[27] It was quoted at length by William James in his *Varieties of Religious Experience*,[28] and Ford had been impressed by it. He tells Trine: "Everything you see now – we have been through it all of it before. We are central stations with myriads of entities going and coming all the time with messages. Thus no one is alone, no one is helpless."[29] In his interview with Viereck, Ford stated his belief in reincarnation and repeated his view of a 'Master Mind' sending "brain waves or messages to us."[30] Some of his sayings elsewhere seem Heraclitean, for example:

> Life, as I see it, is not a location, but a journey. Even the man who most feels himself "settled" is not settled – he is probably sagging back. Everything is in flux, and was meant to be. Life flows. We may live at the same number of the street, but it is never the same man who lives there.[31]

Life is a river which constantly changes its course, and the way of understanding is to follow this river – not the dried up and deserted river bed.[32]

However, his overall philosophical view was Platonist in so far as he attributed an external, independent existence to the abstract thoughts and ideas that occurred to him. He believed that his bright ideas had an external source into which he was tapping. It did not occur to him that his own unique inner development was sufficient to give him these ideas. At heart, he was perhaps a home-loving philosopher who liked nothing better than to sit on his porch at Fair Lane, overlooking the River Rouge, while his wife read out passages from the books he admired.[33]

Much is made nowadays of Ford's anti-Jewish views expressed in a notorious book called *The International Jew* based on a series of 80 articles in *The Dearborn Independent* from May 1920 to January 1922.[34] However it was commonplace after the World War One to blame the war on a conspiracy of international financiers who profited from it, and Ford had picked up this widespread prejudice. Even Ford's friend Thomas Alva Edison got himself into trouble with remarks such as "the Jews were largely responsible for Germany's economic prosperity."[35] Ford probably meant to use this popular prejudice to bolster his faltering political career. However, he abandoned his anti-Jewish campaign after a damaging court case brought by a Jew and as a result he closed *The Dearborn Independent* in 1927.[36] At the same time, he publicly apologized for his campaign. His apology was well received: "Four-fifths of the hundreds of letters addressed to Ford in July 1927 were from Jews, and almost without exception they praised the Industrialist."[37]

In contrast, Adolf Hitler, who had also jumped on the post-war anti-Semitic bandwagon when forming his Nazi party, took these views to their logical conclusion twenty years later, with well-known consequences. There was nothing personal about Ford's views. He had many Jewish friends and he was astonished when one of them protested by returning the Model T gifted to him. Also he employed thousands of Jews in his various factories.[38] When Ford was in his eighties he was reportedly shown newsreels of the atrocities committed in Nazi concentration camps. He was so shocked that he collapsed with a stroke, the last of a series of them.[39]

4. Ford as Visionary and Publicist

Ford's humanistic championship of a people's car began in 1907 when he ordered the planning of an entirely new car.[40] His chief designer, Joseph Galamb recalled: "Early in 1907, Mr. Ford said to me, 'Joe I've an idea to design a new car. Fix a place for yourself on the third floor. Get your board up there and a blackboard'. At that time we didn't know that it was to be the Model T. It was just a new model."[41] Ford's vision for the Model T or 'Tin Lizzie'[42] was as follows:

> I will build a motor car for the great multitude. It will be large enough for the family but small enough for the individual to run and care for. It will be so low in price that no man making a good salary will be unable to own one – and enjoy with his family the blessing of hours of pleasure in God's great open spaces.[43]

Ford brooked no rival to his universal car which was perfected in 1908. In 1912 when he made his first trip to Europe, his engineers thought they would surprise him by building a better car than the Model T. It was superior in appearance and performance and was already attracting orders, but it was not meant for the common man. When Ford returned unexpectedly, he saw the car, walked round it several times and then began tearing it apart with his bare hands. He lambasted his engineers for exceeding his orders and instructed the cancellation of the orders for the new car and for the parts to build it.[44]

Such was the popularity of the Model T that it set the standard for the family saloon car for the rest of the century – four cylinders, four doors and enough room inside for five people. The price was reduced year by year and sales increased year by year.[45] As demand continued to exceed supply, Ford and his men constantly refined their production techniques to increase production and meet the demand. By a trial-and-error process, they developed the assembly line process which was perfected in 1913. This made possible the mass production of cars that doubled the output of his Highland Park factory. Ford indeed said: "Any customer can have a car painted any colour that he wants so long as it is black."[46] But this applied only from 1914 onwards when the mass assembly process made it easier to use one colour. In 1925, they "bowed to the inevitable and brought out the Model T in a choice of colors."[47]

Ford's dramatic increase of his workers' wages in 1914 was borne out of business necessity. Although mass production techniques reduced the cost of making the Model T they also increased the tedium of the job as they enslaved workers to the assembly line. It was increasingly difficult to find skilled workers. The publicity of his announcement ensured that Ford had no difficulty finding workers. Indeed, he succeeded beyond his wildest dreams. "By the middle of January 1914, there were 15,000 desperate men gathering every morning to jam Woodward Avenue and Manchester Street, which led to the Highland Park employment office."[48]

His revolutionary approach to manufacturing brought him world-wide fame and this encouraged him to develop his ideas about business and indeed about everything. He became vain enough to think that he could stop the war, In 1916, he famously sent a 'Peace Ship' to Europe in a foolish attempt to do that.[49] In November 1918, he purchased the weekly newspaper, *The Dearborn Independent*, and employed the Canadian journalist, William J. Cameron, to write "Mr. Ford's Page" in the newspaper. As Ford had "no stomach for writing ... he would dictate his views" to Cameron who "possessed the extraordinary ability to pick up the abrupt, enigmatic remarks that his employer loved to throw out and make sense of them. Henry Ford, it was once said, spoke in telegrams, and it was Cameron's gift to convert these into lucid, flowing sermons of considerable grace and persuasiveness which he set down on paper in *The Dearborn Independent* and, in later years, delivered on the radio ... and never once did the master find cause to rebuke his interpreter for misrepresentation, exaggeration, or embellishment."[50]

Ninety-eight articles for 'Mr. Ford's Page' were republished in a 452 page book, *Ford's Ideals* (1922). In the Preface, Cameron wrote:

> The question has often been asked what part Mr. Ford personally takes in the preparation of 'Mr. Ford's Page'. Every essential part. He supplies the ideas. Very often he supplies the words in which his ideas are set forth. He does not manipulate the typewriter nor does he occupy himself with the detail of seeing the copy through the press, but the entire inspiration, the point of view, the resistless analysis, the ripeness of judgment, are his. Without him there would be no 'Mr. Ford's Page'.[51]

Cameron was able virtually to read Ford's mind and, when he sat with Ford in interviews with journalists, he would break into his conversation and say: "'What Mr. Ford means is...' and then proceed to expound on Ford's views. The manufacturer, as he listened to the flawless presentation of his ideas, would nod pleasantly. Never, so far as his associates knew, did Ford repudiate his aide's comments."[52] As one of Ford's secretaries put it:

> Cameron, for instance, had a personality of his own, but he was one man that Henry Ford absolutely trusted. If it hadn't been for Cameron, Henry Ford would have gotten into some of the damnedest holes you can imagine, politically and nationally, and Cameron saved him time after time.[53]

Sometimes, when on holiday, Ford would call in the reporters and say "Well, I haven't anybody to censor me. I can talk freely." The more extravagant aspects of his thinking would then become apparent:

In 1928, in one interview, he told Boston reporters that the army and navy should enforce Prohibition; that fruit, starch, and proteins should be eaten separately; that 'somewhere there is a Master Mind which sends brain waves or messages to us – the Brain of Mankind, the Brain of the Earth'; that sex did not make the world go round; that the coming generation was too intelligent for another world war; that both Al Smith and Herbert Hoover were good for business. Ford found time in the same interview to discuss airplanes, rubber plants, farming, and the New Bedford textile industry's troubles.[54]

Ford's 'collaboration' with Samuel Crowther in writing his autobiography and other works was similar to that with Cameron. Crowther had more expertise in economics than Cameron and he was able to give more depth to Ford's views. But both Crowther and Cameron were journalists who were more interested in good copy and striking sayings than in working out Ford's ideas systematically. The arguments are more rhetorical than logically coherent. The same applies to other published interviews such as Faurote's interview with Ford published as *My Philosophy of Industry*.[55] Crowther derived his material from his interviews with Ford and his associates such as Cameron. He also used paragraphs and arguments from 'Mr. Ford's Page' material but worked them into his text in a different context.[56]

The view that Ford was merely the front man for men cleverer and better educated than himself was scotched by another of his associates who also sat with him in meetings with journalists, Robert L. Black:

> Whatever they say about Cameron, or about me, or about anybody else, and what *we* did for Mr. Ford – and a lot of people got the idea that he had very astute and smart public relations men or press men – actually, Henry Ford was the top guy as far as creating situations that resulted in some of the top stories... Nobody made Henry Ford from a publicity standpoint except himself; Cameron or any of the rest of us just merely *helped*... This idea that Henry Ford was an ignoramus, and had his smartness due to his public relations men who engineered all his stuff, is *absolutely untrue*. It was a strange combination; he was a very shy man with this amazing sense of publicity values.[57]

Ford's writings were enormously successful and were translated and read all over the world. So dominant was Ford's thinking in the 1920s and 30s, that Aldous Huxley satirized it in his futuristic novel, *Brave New World* (1932), in which Fordism is the prevailing religion with people saying 'Our Ford', 'Oh Ford', 'Thank Ford' and making the sign of T (after the Model T) on their stomachs. Also, the years are dated A.F. or Anno Ford ('In the Year of our Ford') beginning in 1908 when the Model T was first put on the market.[58]

As Ford's thought was expressed in journalistic terms, perhaps the most enduring feature of his thought has been the striking quotations attributed to him. These include the following. "Failure is only the opportunity more intelligently to begin again."[59] "If there is any one secret of success, it lies in the ability to get the other person's point of view and see things from that person's angle as well as from your own." "There is one rule for the industrialist and that is: Make the best quality of goods possible at the lowest cost possible, paying the highest wages possible."[60] Finally, "The highest use of capital is not to make more money, but to make money do more service for the betterment of life."[61]

One of his most notorious sayings is that "history is bunk." But this was an offhand comment made to a *New York Times* journalist in 1919. What he actually said was: "History is more or less the bunk. We want to live in the present, and the only history that is worth a tinker's damn is the history we make today."[62] But he was only against 'history' in the sense of retaining tradition and outmoded ways of thinking about things. In his view, we must not rely on traditional ways but must constantly find new ways of doing things: "If we have a tradition it is this: Everything can always be done better than it is being done."[63] He was not against the teaching of history in schools: "We have history in our schools, but it is the history of evolving the mastery of the means of life."[64]

The popularity of such 'Fordisms' has detracted from the importance of the system of thought inherent in the Fordian writings. It appears that no concerted attempt has been made to organize this thinking into a philosophical system. The following list brings together some of the principal features of Ford's humanist ideas. They show the range of his thought scattered throughout the writings attributed to him. Perhaps they are enough to demonstrate that there is a unified system of thought behind his thinking despite the diffuseness of these writings. They also suggest that much remains to be done to make that system coherent.

5. The Enlightened Nature of Ford's Humanism

1. Increasing wages instead of lowering them.
The world-wide acceptance of Ford's wage policy meant that wages were no longer the subject of cost-cutting to the extent advocated by Carnegian capitalism. Because of Ford's intervention, it became the norm throughout the twentieth century for wages to be increased year by year. Even today, wages are usually only cut when organizations are dire straits and workers willingly accept the cuts to save their organization. It is only recently with the financial crisis that this aspect of humane capitalism is now threatened,

(though perhaps justifiably in the case of highly placed bankers – Ford had no love of bankers![65])

2. Reducing working hours instead of increasing them.

Reducing working hours went along with increasing wages so that Ford was able to proclaim that: "The payment of five dollars a day for an eight-hour day was one of the finest cost-cutting moves we ever made."[66] Workers worked more efficiently as a result and costs were reduced. It is fallacious to assume that reducing the time for work to be done automatically decreases workers' productivity. It forces them to organize their time better so that the same level of productivity can be achieved. More work is done in less time. Ford always emphasized the need to put more thought into work and this usually increases productivity. Moreover, management have to do the thinking as "the work of thinking cannot be delegated."[67]

3. Cutting the working week instead of leaving it as it is.

Before Ford's advances, the industry standard was a "six day week of twelve-hour days"[68] In September 1926, Ford introduced the five day week, eight hours a day[69] and this has become the industrial and commercial norm and remains so to this day. Industry and commerce has now stagnated around this norm although the possibility of a four day week must always exist. Ford recognized this when he stated: "The five-day week is not the ultimate, and neither is the eight-hour day."[70] In doing the same work in four days, workers increase their efficiency and productivity. The leisure industry benefits from this, and diversity is added to the economy. The more diverse the economy is, the more the intensity of activity and therefore the greater the GNP and the standard of living. But this is only possible if people in industry and commerce are prepared to organize themselves strictly enough to increase their efficiency and productivity. Ford was very much against waste and saw the reduction of waste as being an important way to increase efficiency and reduce costs.[71]

4. Increasing workers' leisure time instead of reducing it.

Ford's promotion of leisure time was not just humanitarian. It was good business as happy and fulfilled workers are more efficient, hardworking and reliable. Ford advocated finding a balance in life between work and play. The world used to be divided into those who worked and those who played. It is something new that nowadays we all have to find a balance between these. "Working all the time muddles the brain. Playing all the time muddles the brain."[72] Moreover, Ford did not envisage the total elimination of work in favour of leisure time. He always emphasized the importance of work. Life consists in finding out the work that each of us has to do in the world, or as he put it: "The whole secret of a successful life is to find out what it is one's destiny to do, and then do it."[73] Thus, his view is that the purpose of society is to serve the public by providing the conditions in which each individual can best find out what is their destiny to do. Society should enable them to fulfil that destiny in so far as it is rational, legal, laudable and moral to do so.

5 The Service Principle.
The crux of Ford's humanism lies in the fundamental ideal of giving service to the community:

> The spirit of service is just a knowledge that no man can survive, no industry can survive, no government can survive, no system of civilization can survive which does not continually give service to the greatest possible number. The only interest one can have in anything is the service one gets from it or gives to it.[74]

This might be called a 'service principle' in which *giving service* to the greatest number replaces the utilitarian felicific principle of *giving happiness* to the greatest number. Thus, service must be put before profit:

> Without a profit, business cannot extend. There is nothing inherently wrong about making a profit. Well-conducted business enterprise cannot fail to return a profit, but profit must and inevitably will come as a reward for good service. It cannot be the basis – it must be the result of service.[75]

6. A classless consumer society.
As against class-obsessed Marxism, Ford recognised only one class – the class of consumers that includes everyone. He therefore promoted and popularized the idea of the consumer society. "All are Members of the Consuming Class" is the title of one of his newspaper articles.[76] Therein he argues that the class division between labour and capital is economically inadmissible since the important point is that both are consumers.

> By the law of nature we are all consumers. Rich or poor, learned or ignorant, it does not matter – every living organism consumes the material of life, and for us this means mostly food for the body and the material necessities of residence on the earth.[77]

7. A prosperous society.
Ford defines 'prosperity' in terms of the benefits to society as a whole. A prosperous society does not lie in an increasing number of mega-rich people who acquire an increasing proportion of society's wealth:

A truly prosperous time is when the largest number of people are getting all they can legitimately eat and wear, and are in every sense of the word comfortable. It is the degree of the comfort of the people at large – not the size of the manufacturer's bank balance – that evidences prosperity. The function of the manufacturer is to contribute to this comfort. He is an instrument of society and he can serve society only as he manages his enterprises so as to turn over to the public an increasingly better product at an ever-decreasing price, and at the same time to pay to all those who have a hand in his business an ever-increasing wage, based upon the work they do. In this way and in this way alone can a manufacturer or any one in business justify his existence.[78]

8. The role of capital.

The humane nature of Ford's capitalism is also evident in the following passages:

Capital that is not constantly making conditions of daily labour better and the reward of daily labour more just, is not fulfilling its highest function. The highest use of capital is not to make more money but to make money do more service for betterment of life. Unless we in our industries are helping to solve the social problem, we are not doing our principal work. We are not serving.[79]

The man who is a capitalist and nothing else, who gambles with the fruits of other men's labours, deserves all that is said against him. He is in precisely the same class as the cheap gambler who cheats workingmen out of their wages.[80]

9. The proper use of charity.

Ford thought that charity should be confined to the home and workplace instead of being professionalized and commercialized so that people depend on it and they cease to be self-reliant and self-sufficient. Ford's form of capitalism is frequently called 'Welfare Capitalism'[81] but this is misleading; he would not have subscribed to the Welfare State, European style:

I have no patience with professional charity, or with any sort of commercialized humanitarianism. The moment human helpfulness is systematized, organized, commercialized, and professionalized, the heart of it is extinguished, and it becomes a cold and clammy thing.[82]

If the idea of service be kept in mind, then there is always in every community more work to do than there are men who can do it. Industry organized for service removes the need for philanthropy. Philanthropy, no matter how noble its motive, does not make for self-reliance. We must have

> self-reliance. A community is the better for being discontented, for being dissatisfied with what it has. I do not mean the petty, daily, nagging, gnawing sort of discontent, but a broad, courageous sort of discontent which believes that everything which is done can and ought to be eventually done better. Industry organized for service – and the working-man as well as the leader must serve – can pay wages sufficiently large to permit every family to be both self-reliant and self-supporting. A philanthropy that spends its time and money in helping the world to do more for itself is far better than the sort which merely gives and thus encourages idleness. Philanthropy, like everything else, ought to be productive, and I believe that it can be. I have personally been experimenting with a trade school and a hospital to discover if such institutions, which are commonly regarded as benevolent, cannot be made to stand on their own feet. I have found that they can be.[83]

In his reservations about philanthropy, Ford clearly had Carnegie in mind as well as other philanthropists such as Rockefeller. He did not approve of vast sums of money being accumulated by rapacious capitalists only to be given away in a self-aggrandizing and patronizing manner.

10. The employment of disabled people.

Ford was adamant that work should be found for disabled people instead of excluding them from employment because they are disabled. He was extraordinarily advanced in his insistence that disabled people had work to do in his plants, or even in their homes if necessary. His policy was as follows:

> No one applying for work is refused on account of physical condition. This policy went into effect on January 12, 1914, at the time of setting the minimum wage at five dollars a day and the working day at eight hours. It carried with it the further condition that no one should be discharged on account of physical condition, except, of course, in the case of contagious disease. I think that if an industrial institution is to fill its whole role, it ought to be possible for a cross-section of its employees to show about the same proportions as a cross-section of a society in general.[84]

This was not an act of charity on Ford's part as he was vehemently against charity, as mentioned above:

> It would be quite outside the spirit of what we are trying to do, to take on men because they were crippled, pay them a lower wage, and be content with a lower output. That might be directly helping the men but it would not be helping them in the best way. The best way is always the way by which they can be put on a productive par with able-bodied men. I believe that there is very little occasion for charity in this world – that is, charity in the sense of making gifts.[85]

Thus, Ford's answer to disability allowances and the like must be that these forms of support are not needed because even disabled people can be found work to do provided that organizations work hard enough to find a place for them.

11. Elimination of poverty.
 Ford was of the view that poverty can be eliminated by better organization of industry and commerce on the basis of service instead of the profit motive which regards poverty as the inevitable consequence of survival of the fittest.

> The abolishing of poverty is the only legitimate purpose of business, and its accomplishment is not an impossibility unless we imagine that it can be done all at once by edict.[86]

> There is no way out from poverty except through work... And the hardest of all work must come in the management.[87]

If business organizations were efficiently run on the principle of service, then bottlenecks and bubbles might be prevented which are caused by excessive profit-making, cut-throat competition, excessive use of credit, making money out of money, or lack of waste management. All these factors militate against the efficient organization of industry and commerce, and there would be no need for state interference since the application of humane capitalism as a way of thinking would be sufficient for the purpose. Industry and commerce would be self-regulating on that basis. Clearly, this view needs to be worked in much greater detail to make it feasible.

12. A peaceful world.
Ford was an ardent pacifist as exemplified by his abortive 'Peace Ship' mission mentioned above. However he paid a heavy price for his pacifism. In 1935, Italy had ordered and paid for 800 trucks from Ford Company. Mussolini had planned to use the trucks when he attacked and invaded Ethiopia. When Ford learned of this, he refused delivery of the trucks. Mussolini then imposed restrictions on Ford's Italian business, which was virtually wrecked.[88] In 1940, Ford declined to make engines for British planes as he would not allow military equipment to be made for other countries at war. However, that all changed when the USA entered the war. By 1944, the Ford bomber factory at Ypsilanti, Michigan was producing a bomber every hour.[89]

6. The Relevance of Ford's Humanism Today

As already pointed out, Ford's humane capitalism has never been worked out properly as a system in the way that Adam Smith, for example, worked out his theory of economics in the book *The Wealth of Nations*. As a result, Ford's system is wide open to misinterpretation. Calling it 'welfare capitalism' leads to its being mistakenly confounded with socialism and even communism. Yet, as we have seen, Ford would not have approved of the welfare state, especially the European model. He never countenanced interference by the state in industry and commerce. He wanted people in industry and commerce to work harder and put more thought into what they were doing to serve the community and, in that way, they would alleviate poverty, inequality and other bottlenecks and distortions in society.

In other words, the private sector should take over the provision of welfare and it should not be left to the state. Unfortunately, this view has never caught on as the primacy of profit-making has overridden all thoughts of welfare provision in industry and commerce. In his early court cases, Ford failed to convince the business community that service should come before profit. He clearly thought the word 'market' should apply to the exchange of goods and services involving human beings, and not just to money markets such as the stock, futures, derivatives and commodity markets. These tend to serve Mammon more than the real needs of the public. As a result, making money out of credit transactions has gone beyond human control with consequences now known to all. Ford objected to money being used to make more money without any productive benefit:

> Dealing in money, the commodity of exchange, is a very lucrative business. When money itself becomes an article of commerce to be bought and sold before real wealth can be moved or exchanged, the usurers and speculators are thereby permitted to lay a tax on production. The hold which controllers of money are able to maintain on productive forces is seen to be more powerful when it is remembered that, although money is supposed to represent the real wealth of the world, there is always much more wealth than there is money, and real wealth is often compelled to wait upon money, thus leading to that most paradoxical situation–a world filled with wealth but suffering want.[90]

Fordian capitalism has high economic and humanistic ideals. It aims to benefit people by improving their living standards, increasing wage levels, supplying more and cheaper goods, and adding to the diversity of life by "making money do more service for the betterment of life."[91] The aim of reducing costs and increasing does not exist simply to benefit its shareholders; it is primarily a way of organizing people to benefit both themselves and the public they serve. Thus, capitalism is not exploitation when workers are getting what they want out of it, namely, decent wages, good working conditions, and reasonably fulfilling work. This is clearly what Ford's humane capitalism is all about, however misapplied capitalism in general has been. Good capitalism can oust out bad capitalism by applying the following Fordian principles:

1. Using better technological and managerial techniques to lower costs and eliminate waste.

2. Using cost savings to benefit shareholders, employees, and consumers in a balanced and evenhanded way.

3.   Thus balancing the increases in dividends and wages, with lower prices, and a better service to consumers.

These factors are measurable in accounting and economic terms, so that they might form the basis of a science on the matter. The principles are perhaps as clear and unequivocal as, for instance, Newton's Laws of Motion. At any rate, their benefits have been shown beyond doubt over the past century.

The banking crisis of 2008 resulted from applying false ideas about credit, loans, and money. Ford continually warned about the consequences of overusing credit and using money to make more money in a pyramid fashion. If his strictures had been heeded during the 1920s, the Great Depression might have been averted. Thus, in recent years, banks and other financial organizations have adopted inhumane capitalism by taking such false ideas to their logical extreme. Their ideas have become disconnected from human needs and no longer serve humanity. The making of money through buying and selling derivatives and the like becomes an end in itself and has no relevance to everyday life. There is no trickle down effect with such inhumane capitalism. The same applies when profit-making is pursued dogmatically for the benefit of shareholders and to the absolute detriment of employees and customers.

Humane capitalism also implies that the global economy can be regulated with more humanity, insight and foresight than at present. More effort should be made to correct imbalances, bottlenecks and other distortions which threaten its smooth functioning. Blind market forces can be as blindly destructive as they are blindly progressive. The world economy is self-regulating only in so far as we consciously participate in its regulation. Without that participation, it is no more than a wild beast without civilized control. We can regulate the world economy because we have the knowledge to do so. Its state is known because we have the data and statistics concerning its functioning.

The blanket use of monetary policy only contributes to the imbalances and bottlenecks. The cheapening of money through low interest rates and quantitative easing, increases the vast debt mountain which must tumble sooner or later. Governments need to regulate banking activity to reduce debt provision rather than use monetary policy to increase it. Ford was justly suspicious of bankers who make money out of money without contributing materially to the economy.

The important point is the economy exists to serve the public. It should not be subservient to abstract ideas such as institutional profit, growing GNP, national pride, to the extent that these ideas become more important than people. These ideas are only important when they serve people in obvious ways such as improving their standard of living just as Ford's humane capitalism succeeded in doing during the twentieth century. Whether that form of capitalism can be adapted to serve the twenty-first century equally well remains to be seen.

Notes

1. Henry Ford in collaboration with Samuel Crowther, *My Life and Work* (London: William Heinemann, 1922), p. 253.

2. Carnegie was born in Dunfermline, Fife, UK, as was this author, who therefore inherited a lifelong interest in this character.

3. Andrew Carnegie, *Autobiography* (London: Constable & Co., 1920), p. 339.

4. Andrew Carnegie, "The Advantages of Poverty," in *The Gospel of Wealth, and Other Timely Essays*, ed. Edward C. Kirkland (Cambridge, Mass.: Harvard University Press, 1962), p. 64.

5. Carnegie, *The Gospel of Wealth*, p. 104.

6. Leon Wolf, *Lockout: The Story of the Homestead Strike of 1892* (London: Longmans, Green and Co., 1965), p. 39. The same chapter documents the inhuman conditions which Carnegie's workers endured at Homestead and in their homes.

7. Wolf, *Lockout*, p. 62.

8. George Harvey, *Henry Clay Frick: The Man* (New York: Charles Scribner's Sons, 1928), p. 115.

9. Wolf, *Lockout*, p. 130. Apparently sources differ as to the exact number of men killed.

10. *Ibid.*, p. 107.

11. Congressional Committee: House reports, 2nd session, 52nd Congress 1892–93, vol. 3, Report 2447. As cited by Raymond Lamont-Brown, *Carnegie: 'The Richest Man in the World'* (Stroud, UK: Sutton Publishing Ltd., 2005), ch. 15, p. 144.

12. Carnegie, *Autobiography*, p. 231.

13. Wolf, *Lockout*, p. 101.

14. *Ibid.*, p. 177.

15. Charles E. Sorenson with Samuel T. Williamson, *Forty Years With Ford* (London: Jonathan Cape, 1957), pp. 13–14.

16. *Ibid.*, p. 12.

17. *Ibid.*, p. 24.

18. *Ibid.*, p. 25.

19. *Ibid.*

20. *Ibid.*

21. *Ibid.*, p. 34.

22. David E. Nye, *Henry Ford: "Ignorant Idealist"* (Port Washington, N.Y.: Kennikat Press, 1979), p. 18. This occurred in 1916 during a libel case in which he sued the *Chicago Tribune* for calling him an anarchist. He won the case but received only six cents in damages though he sued for a million dollars.

23. Sorenson, *Forty Years With Ford*, p. 13.

24. Robert Lacey, *Ford: The Men and the Machine* (London: William Heinemann, 1986), p. 161 and 210.

25. David L. Lewis, *The Public Image of Henry Ford* (Detroit: Wayne State University Press, 1976), p. 64.

26. Ford, *My Life and Work*, p. 239.

27. R. W. Trine, *In Tune with the Infinite* (London: G. Bell and Sons, 1916).

28. William James, *The Varieties of Religious Experience* (London: Penguin, 1985), pp. 100–101 and 393–394.

29. R. W. Trine, *The Power That Wins: Henry Ford and Ralph Waldo Trine in an intimate talk on Life, the Inner Things of the Mind and Spirit and the Inner Powers and Forces that make for achievement* (London: Williams & Norgate, 1930), p. 145.

30. George Sylvester Viereck, "The Metaphysics of Henry Ford" in *Glimpses of the Great* (London: Duckworth, 1930), p. 347.

31. Ford, *My Life and Work*, p. 43.

32. Henry Ford, *My Philosophy of Industry*, an authorized interview by Fay Leone Faurote (New York: Forum Publishing Co., 1928); "Why I Believe in Progress," p. 94.

33. Sorenson, *Forty Years With Ford*, p. 16.

34. *The International Jew – The World's Foremost Problem*, by Henry Ford, founder of the Ford Motor Company, and the editors of *The Dearborn Independent* (Dearborn, Mich.: Dearborn Publishing Company, 1922).

35. Matthew Josephson, *Edison* (London: Eyre & Spottiswoode, 1961), p. 465.

36. David L. Lewis, *The Public Image of Henry Ford* (Detroit: Wayne State University Press, 1976), p. 146.

37. *Ibid.*

38. Robert Lacey, *Ford: The Men and the Machine* (London: William Heinemann, 1986), p. 219.

39. Manuscript of Josephine Gomon, Bentley Historical Library, Gomon papers, Box 10, draft manuscript "The Poor Mr Ford." As cited by Lacey, *ibid.*, pp. 218–219.

40. Ford himself uses the word 'car' in his writings at least as often as 'automobile'.

41. "An Interview with Joseph Galamb" in *Tin Lizzie* by Philip Van Doren Stern (New York: Simon and Shuster, 1955), p. 138.

42. It was nicknamed 'Tin Lizzie' apparently because 'Lizzie' was a slang word for a domestic servant and the car became an additional 'tin' servant of the family. See this forum online: http://www.fordbarn.com/forum/showthread.php?t=30549 (retrieved 3-28-2012).

43. Ford, *My Life and Work*, p. 73.

44. "An Interview with George Brown" in *Tin Lizzie*, pp. 140–143. See also Lacey, *Ford: The Men and the Machine*, pp. 288–289.

45. There is a table of prices and production figures for the Model T in *My Life and Work*, p. 146.

46. *My Life and Work*, p. 72.

47. Allan Nevins and Frank Ernest Hill, *Ford: Expansion and Challenge, 1915–1933*. (New York: Charles Scribner's Sons, 1957), p. 400.

48. Lacey, *Ford: The Men and the Machine*, p. 118.

49. *My Life and Work*, p. 245.

50. Lacey, *Ford: The Men and the Machine*, p. 196.

51. *Ford Ideals*: Being a Selection from "Mr. Ford's Page" in *The Dearborn Independent* (Dearborn, Mich.: Dearborn Publishing Company, 1922), pp. 5–6.

52. Lewis, *The Public Image of Henry Ford*, p. 222.

53. From the oral reminiscences of H. M. Cordell, a secretary to Henry Ford, as quoted in *Henry's Lieutenants* by Ford Richardson Bryan (Detroit, Mich.: Wayne State University Press, 1993), p. 53.

54. Lewis, *The Public Image of Henry Ford.*

55. Ford, *My Philosophy of Industry.*

56. "Working from a few interviews with Henry but largely from 'Mr. Ford's Own Page' and conversations with Liebold and Cameron, Crowther crafted a masterpiece of its kind." Lacey, *Ford: The Men and the Machine*, p. 211. I must dispute the "largely from" assumption, since I have found only scattered passages in *Ford Ideals* that are the same or made use of in *My Life and my Work*; for example p. 244 has passages from *Ford Ideals* at p. 86, and p. 266 accords with *Ford Ideals* at p. 39.

57. Robert L. Black, *Reminiscences*, in the Ford Archives in Dearborn, Michigan, p. 158. As quoted by Lewis, *The Public Image of Henry Ford*, p. 217.

58. Aldous Huxley, *Brave New World* (London: Penguin Books, 1964), pp. 31, 34, and 70.

59. *My Life and Work*, p. 19.

60. These last two quotations are widely found in internet lists of Ford's quotations but are yet to be sourced.

61. *My Life and Work*, p. 194.

62. As quoted by Keith Sward, *The Legend of Henry Ford* (New York: Rinehart & Co., 1948), p. 110.

63. *My Life and Work*, p. 98.

64. Henry Ford in collaboration with Samuel Crowther, *Moving Forward* (London: William Heinemann, 1931), p. 271.

65. See for example *My Life and Work*, p. 176: "Bankers play far too great a part in the conduct of industry."

66. *My Life and Work*, p. 147.

67. *Moving Forward*, p. 305.

68. *Ibid.*, p. 63. However, Ford's introduction of round-the-clock eight hour shifts was preceded by two nine-hour shifts per day – see Lacey, *Ford: The Men and the Machine*, p. 117.

69. *Ibid.*, p. 80.

70. *Ibid.*, p. 88.

71. *Ibid.*, p. 19; ibid., pp. 87–90; Ford, *Today and Tomorrow* (London: William Heinemann, 1926), pp. 89–98; *Moving Forward*, p. 220–241, etc.

72. Ford, *Today and Tomorrow*, p. 221.

73. Ford, *My Philosophy of Industry*, p. 75.

74. *Today and Tomorrow*, p. 269.

75. *My Life and Work*, p. 20. These rules are restated and re-affirmed at p. 278, and in *Moving Forward* at pp. 174–175.

76. See *Ford Ideals*, p. 249.

77. *Ford Ideals*, pp. 249–250.

78. *My Life and Work*, pp. 134–135.

79. *Ibid.*, p. 194.

80. *Ibid.*, p. 254.

81. See for instance his biography in www.wikipedia.org.

82. *My Life and Work*, p. 206–207.

83. *Ibid.*, pp. 209–210.

84. *Ibid.*, pp. 106–107.

85. *Ibid.*, p. 107.

86. *Moving Forward*, p.106.

87. *Today and Tomorrow*, pp. 269–70.

88. Allan Nevins and Frank Ernest Hill, *Ford: Decline and Rebirth, 1933–1962* (New York: Charles Scribner's Sons, 1962), p. 104.

89. Edward Keller, *Mr. Ford – What Have You Done? Henry Ford's Views on Economics* (Qulin, Misouri: Keaton Keller, 1993), pp. 70–71.

90. *My Life and Work*, p. 182.

91.   *Ibid.*, p. 194.

References

Bachelor, Ray. 1994. *Henry Ford: Mass Production, Modernism and Design*. Manchester, UK: Manchester University Press.

Bryan, Ford Richardson. 1993. *Henry's Lieutenants*. Detroit, Mich.: Wayne State University Press.

Carnegie, Andrew. 1900. *The Gospel of Wealth, and Other Timely Essays*, ed. Edward C. Kirkland. Cambridge, Mass.: Harvard University Press, 1962.

Carnegie, Andrew. 1920. *Autobiography*. London: Constable & Co.

Ford, Henry. 1922. *The International Jew – The World's Foremost Problem*. Dearborn, Mich.: Dearborn Publishing Company.

Ford, Henry. 1922. "Being a Selection from 'Mr. Ford's Page'," in the *Dearborn Independent*. Dearborn, Mich.: Dearborn Publishing Company.

Ford, Henry. 1922. *My Life and Work*, in collaboration with Samuel Crowther. London: William Heinemann.

Ford, Henry. 1926. *Today and Tomorrow*, in collaboration with Samuel Crowther. London: William Heinemann.

Ford, Henry. 1928. *My Philosophy of Industry*, interview by Fay Leone Faurote. New York: Forum Publishing Co.

Ford, Henry. 1931. *Moving Forward*, in collaboration with Samuel Crowther. London: William Henemann.

Harvey, George. 1928. *Henry Clay Frick: The Man*. New York: Charles Scribner's Sons.

Huxley, Aldous. 1932. *Brave New World*. London: Penguin, 1964.

James, William. 1902. *The Varieties of Religious Experience*. London: Penguin, 1985.

Josephson, Matthew. *Edison*. London: Eyre & Spottiswoode, 1961.

Keller, Edward. 1993. *Mr. Ford – What Have You Done? Henry Ford's Views on Economics*. Qulin, Misouri: Keaton Keller.

Lacey, Robert. 1986. *Ford: The Men and the Machine*. London: William Heinemann.

Lamont-Brown, Raymond. 2005. *Carnegie: 'The Richest Man in the World'*. Stroud, UK: Sutton Publishing.

Lewis, David L. 1976. *The Public Image of Henry Ford*. Detroit, Mich.: Wayne State University Press.

Nevins, Allan, and Frank Ernest Hill. 1954. *Ford: The Times, the Man, the Company*. New York: Charles Scribner's Sons.

Nevins, Allan, and Frank Ernest Hill. 1957. *Ford: Expansion and Challenge, 1915–1933*. New York: Charles Scribner's Sons.

Nevins, Allan, and Frank Ernest Hill. 1962. *Ford: Decline and Rebirth, 1933–1962*. New York: Charles Scribner's Sons.

Nye, David E. 1979. *Henry Ford: "Ignorant Idealist."* Port Washington, N.Y.: Kennikat Press.

Sorenson, Charles E., with Samuel T. Williamson. 1957. *Forty Years With Ford*. London: Jonathan Cape.

Stern, Philip Van Doren. 1955. *Tin Lizzie*. New York: Simon and Shuster.

Sward, Keith. 1948. *The Legend of Henry Ford*. New York: Rinehart & Co.

Trine, Ralph Waldo. 1899. *In Tune with the Infinite*. London: G. Bell and Sons, 1916.

Trine, Ralph Waldo. 1930. *The Power That Wins, Henry Ford and Ralph Waldo Trine in an intimate talk on Life, the Inner Things of the Mind and Spirit and the Inner Powers and Forces that make for Achievement*. London: Williams & Norgate.

Viereck, George Sylvester. 1930. "The Metaphysics of Henry Ford," in *Glimpses of the Great* (London: Duckworth), pp. 342–355.

Wolf, Leon. 1965. *Lockout: The Story of the Homestead Strike of 1892.* London: Longmans, Green and Co.

Part Four

Posterity

IX. Posterity—An Eighteenth Century Answer to God and Religion

The French *philosophes* of the eighteenth century had a big problem. They no longer believed in Christianity or the Holy Catholic Church. They had no time for revelation, ritual, or the priesthood. Heaven and hell were here on Earth and nowhere else. In their view, organized religion had to be vanquished but they wished to save the spirit of morality from the wreckage. And they thought that humans could be moral in seeking honor and glory. All of these topics were addressed in their *Encyclopédie* (published 1751 onwards) in articles by Denis Diderot (1713-84), Étienne Bonnot de Condillac (1715-80), Jean D'Alembert (1717-83), Baron D'Holbach (1723-89), and Jean-François Marmontel (1723-99), in which they all eagerly sought a rational substitute for religion. They believed that people didn't need religion—that the future benefits of behaving themselves and acting morally were motivation enough. Society in the future would be a better one when everyone sought their own good instead of being indoctrinated by a religious morality that perpetuated a medieval mentality. Thus, Marmontel in his *Encyclopédie* article on glory said: "Morality should take the example of theology, and fortify virtue against the scorn and ingratitude of men, by showing it in the distance a happier time and a juster world."[1]

Diderot in particular considered posterity to be a worthy replacement for God and religion. In the absence of any heavenly reward for living a moral life, the only compensation for Diderot was the possibility of living forever in the memory of future generations. He argued:

> Do you not see that the judgment of posterity anticipated is the sole encouragement, the sole support, the sole consolation of men in a thousand unhappy circumstances? . . . All these philosophers, these men of integrity who have been the victims of stupid people, of atrocious priests, of enraged tyrants, what consolation remains to them in the hour of death? This: that prejudice passes, and that posterity will transfer to their enemies the ignominy which they have suffered."[2]

He concluded therefore that "posterity for the philosopher is the other world of the man of religion."[3] Also "if our predecessors have done nothing for us, and if we do nothing for our descendants, it is almost in vain that nature wills that man should be perfectible."[4] In this way, Diderot substituted the worship of God with a humanist regard for the future of humankind.

Carl Becker in his book, *The Heavenly City of the Eighteenth-Century Philosophers* (1932), argues that the *philosophes* were creating a so-called Heavenly City in the future in place of Augustine's City of God. He also contends that they were more medieval in their thinking than they realized.[5] However Becker provides no evidence that the *philosophes* used such terms or made such arguments. Moreover it is surely absurd to say that in looking forward to posterity they were also harking back to the Middle Ages, especially as they regarded posterity as being different and potentially better than the present. It would be truer to say that they rationalized the Christian ideal of the Kingdom of God or Heaven replacing it with the prospect of future generations having a better life than their ancestors. In this way of thinking, the human replaces the divine and we are more concerned about human posterity than about non-existent alien or supernatural beings.

H.G. Wells clarified this matter in a 1902 Royal Institution lecture called "The Discovery of the Future." Wells distinguished two types of mind: the first hardly thinks of the future at all, while the second thinks about it constantly and "of present things mainly in relation to the results that must arise from them." He continues:

> The former type of mind, when one gets it in its purity, is retrospective in habit, and it interprets the things of the present, and gives value to this and denies it to that, entirely in relation to the past. The latter type of mind is constructive in habit, it interprets the things of the present and gives value to this and that, entirely in relation to the things designed or foreseen.[6]

A "retrospectivist" turn of mind can therefore be distinguished from a "prospectivist" one. Only the latter really appreciates the value of posterity. Thus, the eighteenth century *philosophes* had a prospectivist viewpoint, which marked a distinct advance on the medieval thinking Becker attempts to pin on them.

Whereas retrospectivists dwell in the past, prospectivists aim to bring the past to the attention of future generations. The latter view is inclusive of all the achievements of humanity including religion. Prospectivists think about these things in relation to their future reception rather than simply recreating the past. They look forward to better things rather than looking to the past as always being preferable to the present or the future. Retrospectivists see the past as a golden age to be eternally reverenced rather than improved upon. Insofar as the Roman Catholic Church is against all change, it is retrospective in its thinking. It constantly recreates the past in the present without thinking of the future as being any different, let alone better. The prospective view would be to think about how future generations can benefit from knowledge of Catholicism—its merits as well as its faults. Thus, religion becomes more a matter of study and contemplation than rigid adherence and unquestioned devotion.

The *philosophes'* disregard for established religion and their regard for posterity influenced the French Revolution and its dechristianization movement, which led to the establishment of the Cult of Reason in 1792, intended to supplant the Roman Catholic Church entirely. Even Robespierre invoked the spirit of posterity in the following speech before the Jacobin Club:

> O posterity, sweet and tender hope of humanity, thou art not a stranger to us; it is for thee that we brave all the blows of tyranny; it is thy happiness which is the price of our painful struggles: often discouraged by the obstacles that surround us, we feel the need of thy consolations; it is to thee that we confide the task of completing our labors, and the destiny of all the unborn generations of men! . . . Make haste, O posterity, to bring to pass the hour of equality, of justice, of happiness! [7]

One might wonder how Robespierre could have sat at his desk signing away the lives of hundreds of innocent people and not considered how bad this would look to future generations. In the end it was his deism that prevented a wholehearted commitment to posterity. "Atheism is aristocratic," he declared, whereas "a great Being who watches over oppressed innocence, and punishes successful crime, is democratic through and through."[8] Influenced by Rousseau's religious views in *Émil*,[9] and by the 'civil religion' of the *Social Contract*,[10] Robespierre established the Cult of the Supreme Being in 1794 to replace the Cult of Reason. Rousseau was his prophet and the *Social Contract* was his bible. He was the high priest of this movement which provided all the answers as far as he was concerned.

Under Robespierre's diktat, atheists (as they had an 'aristocratic' view) were more in danger of the guillotine than Roman Catholic priests, whom he saw as being less of a threat to his views. He thought he was doing the work of God, just as Hitler thought that his persecution of Jews was what he called "God's work." Posterity didn't matter to Robespierre as long as he was intuitively confident that he was serving his god. However, his austere religion of virtue was markedly less popular with the Parisian public than the Cult of Reason. At the first Festival of the Supreme Being, Robespierre was so enthusiastic and full of himself that one of his colleagues exclaimed: "Look at the b****r; it's not enough for him to be master, he has to be God!"[11] This happened on June 8, 1794, and a mere seven weeks later on July 28, Robespierre had his own appointment with Madame Guillotine.

As Madame Roland (1754-1793) put it: "The cowards, they entered into a compromise with guilt! It was decreed that they should fall in their turn; but they fall ingloriously, pitied by no one, and with nothing to hope for from posterity, but its perfect contempt."[12] She bravely and consistently protested against the excesses of the Reign of Terror and when she was guillotined in her turn, she famously remarked: "Oh Liberty, what crimes are committed in thy name!"[13]

Robespierre's re-introduction of God worship paved the way for Napoleon to re-instate the Catholic religion by the Concordat of 1801. Only in 1905 did France return to the secular ideals of the Revolution when a policy of *laïcité* (secularism) was established with the Law on the Separation of the Churches and State, and the rest is modern history.

Notes and References

1. Marmontel in his *Encyclopédie* article on glory, namely, "Gloire" in *Encyclopédie, ou dictionnaire raisonné des sciences, des arts et des métiers* (*Encyclopaedia, or a Systematic Dictionary of the Sciences, Arts, and Crafts*) 1751 - 1772, vol. 7, pp. 716–721.

2. *Œuvres Complètes de Diderot*, (Paris: Éditeur: J. Assézat et M. Tourneux; Maison d'édition: Garnier, 1875-77), Volume XVIII, 'Lettres à Étienne Maurice Falconet' (1716 -1791), Février 1766, pp. 102, 100:

[p.102] Est-ce que vous ne voyez pas que le jugement anticipé de la postérité est le seul encouragement, la seule consolation, l'unique resource de l'homme en mille circonstances malheureuses?
[p. 100] Et ces philosophes, et ces ministres, et ces homes véridiques qui ont été la victime des peoples stupides, des prêtres atroces, des tyrans enrages, quelle consolation leur restait-il en mourant? C'est que le préjugé passerait et que la postérité reverserait l'ignominie sur leur ennemis.

3. *Ibid.*, p. 101. "La postérité pour le philosophe, c'est l'autre monde de l'homme religieux."

4. *Ibid.*, p. 179: "Si nos prédécesseurs n'avaient rien fait pour nous, et si nous ne faisons rien pour nos neveux, ce serait Presque en vain que la nature eût voulu que l'homme fût perfectible."

5. Carl L. Becker, *The Heavenly City of the Eighteenth-Century Philosophers* (1932, New Haven: Yale University Press, 1965), ch. IV, 'The Uses of Posterity', p. 128f.

6. H.G. Wells, *The Discovery of the Future*, ed. by P. Parrinder, (London: PNL Press, 1989), p. 19. (Available at http://www.archive.org/details/discoveryoffutur00well (*Accessed 2014-12-21*)

7. Cf. Charles Vellay, *Discours et rapports de Robespierre*, (Paris: Librairie Charpentier et Fasquelle, 1908), pp. 155, 156. Also,

Journal des débats de la société des amis de la constitution (January, 1792), No. 127, p.3. French text as follows :

> Doux et tendre espoir de l'humanité, postérité naissante, tu ne nous es point étrangère; c'est pour toi que nous affrontons tous les coups de la tyrannie; c'est ton bonheur qui est le prix de nos pénibles combats: découragés souvent par les objets qui nous environnent, nous sentons le besoin de nous élancer dans ton sein; c'est à toi que nous confions le soin d'achever notre ouvrage, et la destinée de toutes les générations d'hommes qui doivent sortir du néant! . . . [p.156] Postérité naissante, hâte-toi de croître et d'amener les jours de l'égalité, de la justice et du bonheur!

8. Cf. François Victor Alphonse Aulard (1849 – 1928), *Le Culte de la Raison et le Culte de l'Être Suprême 1793-94*, (Paris: Ancienne Librairie Germer Ballièhe, Félix Algan, Éditeur, 1892), ch. XVI, p. 215:

> L'athéisme est aristocratique. L'idée d'un grand Être qui veille sur l'innocence opprimée et qui punit le crime triumphant est toute populaire.

9. Jean-Jacques Rousseau, *Émil*, (1762), trans, Barbara Foxley, (London: Dent – Everyman's Library, 1969), 'The Creed of a Sayorard Priest', pp. 228-278. The French original: *Émil ou de l'Éducation,* (Paris: Garnier-Flammerion, 1966), Livre Quatrième, 'Profession de Foi du Vicaire Savoyard', pp. 345-409.

10. Jean-Jacques Rousseau, *The Social Contract*, (1762), trans. G..D.H. Cole, (London: Dent – Everyman's Library, 1966), Book IV, Ch. VIII, 'Civil Religion', p. 106-115. The French original: *Du Contract Social*, (Paris: Garnier-Flammerion, 1966), Livre IV, Ch. VIII,'De la Religion Civile', pp. 170-180.

11. "Voyez ce bougre-là; ce n'est pas assez d'être le maître, il faut encore qu'il soit un dieu!" This was reportedly said by Jacques-Alexis Thuriot (1753–1829). See Joachim Vilate (1767-1795), *Les Mystères de la Mère de Dieu, dévoilés*, Troisième Volume - des Causes secrètes de la Révolution du 9 au 10 Thermidor. (Paris, L'An Troisième de la République Française, [1795]), Ch. XV, p. 64. Also, David Andress, *The Terror*, (New York: Farrar, Straus and Giroux, 2007), p. 310.

12. Madame Marie-Jeanne Roland (1754-1793), *An Appeal to Impartial Posterity*, (*Appel à l'Impartiale Postérité*), (London: printed for J. Johnson, St. Paul's Church-Yard, 1796), Vol I, Part II, 'My Last Thoughts', p. 117. Original French version: *Appel à l'Impartiale Postérité, par la citoyenne Roland, Femme du Ministre de l'Intérieur,* (Paris : Louvet, Maison Egalité, [1795]) 'Mes Dernières Pensèes', p. 79:

Ils ont temporisé avec le crime, les laches! Ils devoient tomber à leur tour; mais ils succombent honteusement sans être plaints de personne, et sans autre perspective, dans la posterité, que son parfait mépris.

13. Cf. Alphonse de Lamartine, *Histoire des Girondines*, (Paris: Furne et C.W. Coquebert, 1847), Volume VII, Book 51, ch. 8, p. 243: "O Liberté, que de crimes on commet en ton nom!" This sentence appears in the following passage:

Après l'exécution de Lamarche, qu'elle entendit sans pâlir, elle monta légèrement les degrés de l'échafaud, et, s'inclinant du côté de la statue de la Liberté comme pour la çonfesser encore en mourant par elle : « O Liberté! » s'écria-t-elle, « O Liberté! que de crimes on commet en ton nom! » Elle se livra à l'exécuteur, et sa tête roula dans le panier.

After the execution of Lamarche which she heard without flinching, she went leisurely up the steps of the scaffold, and, bowing toward the Statue of Liberty as if to confess even dying by it: "O Liberty!" she cried, "O Liberty! What crimes are committed in thy name!" She gave himself up to the executioner and her head rolled into the basket.

X. Does Posterity Watch Over Us?

Always behave as though you were being watched. He is a prudent man who realizes that he is being observed, or will be observed. He knows that walls have ears and that evil deeds are bursting to come out into the light of day. Even when he is alone he behaves as though the eyes of the whole world were upon him, for he realizes that everything will eventually come to light: he regards people who will later hear of his deeds as already witnesses of them. The man who would like the whole world to see inside his home will not be a prey to misgivings just because others can observe him from theirs.

Baltasar Gracián, *The Oracle*, (1647)[1]

If there is a posterity awaiting us in the future, we can be reasonably sure that it will be ubiquitous and all-seeing. We don't need God watching over us when we can imagine posterity doing so. Atheists can cheerfully dispense with God as there are more rational arguments for believing in an ever-vigilant posterity than there are for believing in the existence of an alien being having supernatural abilities to observe us right now. We can extrapolate such future possibilities more rationally than we can supernatural ones. This is because we can imagine future generations having greater knowledge and technological abilities than ourselves, just as we know that our scientific knowledge and technological abilities are better than those of past generations. Such a view doesn't even depend on human race surviving into the future since life is almost certainly springing up throughout the universe on countless planets in countless galaxies. It is part of the universe's complexification process that matter becomes increasing complex in its internal structure. The creation of complex life-forms is a natural consequence of that process, so that life is bound to emerge somewhere at some time.[2] We are already discovering planets which may have the ability to generate life and these discoveries are now raising such possibilities into certainties. Thus, posterity in the form of intelligent beings in future having access to information about our lives is rationally justifiable because it appeals to scientific evidence which is ever accumulating in favour of this viewpoint as compared with the continued lack of evidence for any deity that created the universe or intervenes in it.

The notion of a superior being who is with us all the time and who is present everywhere only makes sense as a way of heralding the scarcely imaginable abilities of posterity to reconstruct the past and to understand present events better than we do ourselves who are living through them. That our lives will be available to the scrutiny of posterity means that they may be even more meaningful in the future than they are in the present. They will read more into our lives than we do ourselves. It is possible that they will have cognisance of our most intimate thoughts and acts. 'Heaven' is what posterity has in store for us in making our lives even more meaningful than they seem to us during our own lifetime. 'Hell' would then be the negative judgments that they make about us and our lives. This view of heaven and hell may seem dream-like but it is a real possibility nevertheless. Even our wildest dreams might be fulfilled if only we had the theoretical knowledge or technological ability needed to fulfil them. Though a person's life might seem meaningless in present day terms, it is perfectly possible that it will be much more meaningful to posterity in the far future, assuming of course that intelligent life of some kind does survive into that very distant future.

It seems certain therefore that our lives will always be there to be watched. The idea of the ubiquity of God palls before the idea of the ubiquitous vigilance of posterity. The former idea is updated by the latter one which is more consonant with scientific knowledge. That our acts are subject to perpetual surveillance has been recognised since the earliest times. For example, in Plato's dialogue, *Phaedrus,* Socrates warns the lusty youth sitting beside him under a plane tree that the cicadas above are witnesses to whatever deeds they observe and that they report their findings directly to the Muses.[3] He implies that we should not give way to our inclinations without considering how our deeds would appear to any watchers. A consciousness of unknown and unseen witnesses to our most intimate acts has been with us since the time we acquired the imagination to think of things not really being what they are immediately perceived to be. Thus, gods, spirits, demons, and angels were posited as possible witnesses of everything we do. Having a better developed scientific imagination than our ancestors, we can now assign this possibility to the future where the ability to reconstruct the past will be a distinct possibility, given the requisite theoretical knowledge and technological know-how. Perhaps we should therefore take Baltasar Gracián's advice and *"Always behave as though you were being watched"* as is quoted in full above.

Thus, our lives themselves may be immortal even if our consciousness certainly is not. Even if we vanish altogether into the void of eternity when we die, we leave our lives behind. That we have lived our lives is an indisputable fact that can be verifiable by all the physical changes we have made during lives, all the work we have done, all the artefacts we have created, all the people who remember us, and all documentation we leave behind us. Nothing and no one can erase the fact of our having lived our lives. It is a question of just how much of our lives can physically survive our demise. However, it is arguable that our lives as a whole are left behind for possible inspection in the future.

Our scientific knowledge now assures us with some certainty that our lives are imprinted all around our environment. Every event has effects of which we are only partially aware through perception and through our current technology, such as microscopes, telescopes, x-rays and so on. We can extrapolate from what we can do now to what improved technology may be capable of in the future. Their technology will simply be more advanced that we can possibly imagine. Though we don't yet know what technology could achieve such effects we can at least imagine their possibility.

Without doubt, more is going on than we are currently able to understand or record with our current science and technology. The events we are presently experiencing may be recorded in the atoms and molecules of our bodies, or in the air, floor, walls, furniture or buildings. Though these changes in the atoms and molecules are currently not detectable by our current technology, they will survive our extinction. It is not beyond the bounds of possibility that the technology of future beings will enable them to reconstruct these recorded events from the atoms and molecules that were formerly in our bodies, the air, water and so on. In that way, the imprints of our lives could be read like a book.

As CCTV cameras are everywhere these days, it is easier than ever to imagine that we are always being watched. Thus, for all we know, posterity may be with us here and now in the sense of their knowing what we are and what we are doing, just as historians know from diaries and journals who people were and what they were doing at a certain time in the past. They will want to do so because they are interested in the past just as we are at present interested in the events in our past. The most insignificant details will be intriguing to them in the same way that an archaeologist today might pore over the remains and artefacts of an obscure peasant who in his day was the lowest of the lowest. Such data are important to the archaeologist because every aspect of people's past lives is interesting and invaluable for the accurate reconstruction of how people lived in the past.

Even if the human race disappears altogether in the future, intelligent beings of some sort somewhere will almost certainly be around. Thus, posterity in the widest sense could access our past. They will look back and see us in the past so that they will be in a sense 'present' in our past. Their presence would therefore be that of a spectator. The presence of posterity is therefore not a physical, or even a ghostly or supernatural presence.

Unless time travel becomes a real possibility, people living in the future are here with us only in that they will have access to knowledge about what we were doing at a certain point in their past. In that way they are able to reconstruct in visual form, by means of an advanced 'virtual reality', the scenes and events in which we ourselves are living our lives at this very moment. They may virtually get inside our skins and feel and think what we are feeling and thinking, here and now. Even today we can read Samuel Pepys's diary and get a sense of living his life from day to day in the 1660s. (His life-style was extraordinarily complex, varied and busy, and it surely gives the lie to the idea that past lifestyles were simpler than those of today!) But we are only imagining what life was like for him. Similarly, people in the future will be on the outside looking in and they will not change events here and now. They will be unable to make us feel or think things or to influence us into doing anything other than what we are actually doing at the present time.

I argue therefore that we can be reasonably certain that sooner or later the ability to observe the past will be developed. The past will be more accurately reconstructed than we can imagine at the moment. The abilities of advanced beings in the future are only possibilities in the sense that the future is uncertain. If advanced beings evolve in the future then the nature of being advanced implies that, sooner or later, they will acquire the abilities of ubiquitous vigilance. No one can be absolutely sure that this will not be the case at sometime in the future. We may assume that future progress will make all these things possible, even though it may take thousands or even millions of years.

Therefore it is only a matter of time when we will be brought before the tribunal of posterity. The Great Day of Judgment awaits us all in posterity wherein we will all be judged according to what we have or have not done in our lives. We will not be personally called before the tribunal of posterity to account for our failings, but our lives will be. In leaving these lives behind us to be judged by in the future, we can never be sure how they will be judged. But we can be sure that we will leave traces behind us of our having lived, and of how we lived, and that these traces may be sufficient to enable our lives to be evaluated one way or another.

We therefore have no need for religion when we have posterity peering at us. We can speculate about the godlike abilities of more advanced, superior beings in the future without needing to believe in their actual existence. There is no point in worshipping them or putting them on a pedestal since they cannot do anything for us that we cannot do for ourselves. Thus, our freewill is unaffected and there is no need for religion whatsoever. We are all personally responsible for our thoughts and deeds and are answerable to posterity for them if not to our fellow human beings. Consequently, there are moral implications in believing in an ever watchful posterity when we take into account the effects and value of our thoughts and deeds from the point of view of posterity.

It may be argued that the universe will come to nothing in the end so there is no point in speculating about posterity and the abilities of advanced beings. According to the laws of thermodynamics, the universe is running down and it will lose all its energy in a 'heat death' which is predicted sometime in the far future. Some people see this as a reason for despair. The universe will come to nothing therefore our lives are worthless. However, the fixed amount of energy available in the universe according to thermodynamics is not necessarily a foregone conclusion. Perhaps additional energy might be brought into existence through the manipulation of black holes, the medium of wormholes or some other means presently unknown to us. Intelligent beings in the far future may acquire the knowledge and technology needed to prolong the existence of the universe or even create a new universe into which life can be transported. Perhaps that is how the present universe came into being in the first place, for all we know at the moment.

In this way, future knowledge can save us from denigrating ourselves into total insignificance. We must invest in the future in that regard by supporting whatever expensive research is required to gain greater understanding of the universe both at the macroscopic and microscopic levels. Cosmological understanding is linked at a very deep level with quantum understanding, since the universe began at that infinitely small level of existence. Indeed, the very fact that we can conduct such research and gain an astonishing amount of information about the universe, near and far, is testimony to our superior and perhaps unique abilities in that regard. No other species on Earth has come close to such achievements, and no other species can be relied upon to do so in the future.

Thus, the after-life, according to the above view, is what awaits our lives after we have left them. Nothing of the present time is lost to the future because it is indelibly imprinted in the atoms and molecules in ourselves and our surroundings. Whatever we do now continues to exist for eternity. This is surely more believable than any religious doctrine as it is based on our present scientific knowledge and on a rational extrapolation from what is now possible to what might be possible in the future.

Finally, in directing ourselves towards posterity, we are adopting a 'prospective' viewpoint that looks to making the future better and is no longer retrospectively reconstructing the past in the future (as is mentioned in the previous section entitled 'Posterity – An 18th Century Answer to God and Religion'). There is no need to stick to religious beliefs as if they were the be-all and end-all of existence. Everything will doubtless make more sense to posterity than it makes to ourselves at present. Hence the need to ensure that there are future generations who will benefit from what we do now. We have the purpose of serving these imagined needs of posterity. They could well be looking back and criticising our failure to do or not to do what we know we should or should not be doing. So watch out!

Notes and References

1. Baltasar Gracián, (1601-1658), *The Oracle: A Manual of the Art of Discretion*, (1647) (London: Dent – Everyman's Library, 1962), §297, pp. 273-275:

[The original Spanish text] *Obrar siempre como a vista.* Aquél es varón remirado que mira que le miran o que le mirarán. Sabe que las paredes oyen, y que lo mal hecho revienta por salir. Aun cuando solo, obra como a vista de todo el mundo, porque sabe que todo se sabrá: ya mira como a testigos ahora a los que por la noticia lo serán después. No se recataba de que le podían registrar en su casa desde las ajenas, el que deseaba que todo el mundo le viese.

2. The complexification process involved in creating ever more complex beings is discussed in greater detail in my book on dualist theory: *The Promise of Dualism.*

3. Plato, *Phaedrus,* (London: Penguin, 1973), 259, pp. 69-70.

Index of Names